iPhone®
FOR
DUMMIES®
A Wiley Brand

Pocket Edition

by Edward C. Baig and Bob LeVitus

D0465342

FOR
DUMMIES®
A Wiley Brand

iPhone® For Dummies®, Pocket Edition

Published by
John Wiley & Sons, Inc.
111 River Street
Hoboken, NJ 07030-5774
www.wiley.com

Copyright © 2014 by John Wiley & Sons, Inc., Hoboken, New Jersey

Published by John Wiley & Sons, Inc., Hoboken, New Jersey

Published simultaneously in Canada

Table of Contents

Introduction

• •

As with most products coming out of Apple, the iPhone is beautifully designed and intuitive to use. And although our editors may not want us to reveal this dirty little secret, the truth is that you'll get pretty far just by exploring the iPhone's many functions and features on your own.

But this book is chock-full of solid information and good advice for getting started with your iPhone. We try to give you a thorough tour of the phone and show you how to sync your data, make calls, control your iPhone with your voice, send text messages, surf the Internet, send e-mail, take pictures, play music, watch videos, and download iPhone apps from the App Store. We hope you have a great time getting familiar with your iPhone.

Icons Used in This Book

Little icons appear in the left margins throughout this book. Consider these icons miniature road signs, telling you something extra about the topic at hand or hammering a point home. Here's what the four icons indicate:

These are the juicy morsels and shortcuts that can make the task at hand faster or easier.

This icon emphasizes the stuff we think you ought to retain. You may even jot down a note to yourself in the iPhone.

Put on your propeller beanie hat and pocket protector — this text includes the truly geeky stuff. You can safely ignore this material; but we include it because it's interesting or informative.

You wouldn't intentionally run a stop sign, would you? In the same fashion, ignoring warnings may be hazardous to your iPhone and (by extension) your wallet.

Where to Go from Here

Why straight to Chapter 1, of course (without passing Go).

One final note: At the time we wrote this book, the information it contained was accurate for all iPhone models (including the 3GS, 4, 4S, 5, and 5s/5c), the latest version of the iPhone OS operating system (iOS 7), and the latest version of iTunes (11). Apple is likely to introduce a new iPhone model or new versions of the operating system and iTunes between book editions. If you've bought a new iPhone or your version of iTunes looks a little different, be sure to check out what Apple has to say at www.apple.com/iphone.

Chapter 1

iPhone Basic Training

. . . .

In This Chapter

▶ Taking a tour of the iPhone

▶ Getting used to the multitouch interface

▶ Trying out Cut, Copy, Paste, and Replace

▶ Checking out Spotlight Search

. . . .

*I*n addition to being a killer cell phone, the iPhone 5s (and its less-expensive brother, the iPhone 5c) is a gorgeous widescreen video iPod, a convenient 8-megapixel camera/camcorder, and a small, powerful Internet communications device. With iPhone apps, your iPhone becomes a PDA, an e-book reader, a handheld gaming device, a memory jogger, an exercise assistant, and ever so much more.

In the following sections, we help you get familiar with this dynamite little device.

Technical Specifications

Before we proceed, here's a list of everything you need before you can actually *use* your iPhone:

✔ An iPhone 5s or 5c

✔ In the United States, a wireless contract with AT&T, Sprint, or Verizon

✔ An Apple ID (which you can set up for free)

✔ Internet access (required) — broadband wireless Internet access recommended

Plus you need one of the following:

✔ A Mac with a USB 2.0 port; OS X version 10.8 or later (some features require OS X Mavericks); and iTunes 11 or later

✔ A PC with a USB 2.0 port; Windows 7 or Windows 8, Windows Vista, or Windows XP Home or Professional with Service Pack 3 or later; and iTunes 11 or later

A Quick Tour Outside

The iPhone is a harmonious combination of hardware and software — read on.

On the top

Here's what you'll find on the top of your iPhone (see Figure 1-1):

✔ **The Sleep/Wake button:** Used to lock or unlock your iPhone and to turn it on or off. When locked, your iPhone can still receive calls and text messages (as well as take pictures with the Camera app), but nothing happens if you touch its screen. When your iPhone is turned off, all incoming calls go directly to voicemail.

On the bottom

Here's what you'll find on the bottom of your iPhone (see Figure 1-2):

Sleep/Wake button

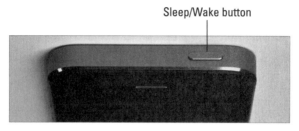

Figure 1-1: The top side of the iPhone 5s.

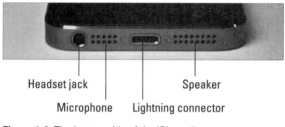

Headset jack   Speaker

Microphone   Lightning connector

Figure 1-2: The bottom side of the iPhone 5s.

- ✔ **Headset jack:** Lets you plug in the included iPhone headset, which has a microphone and remote so that you can talk as well as listen.

- ✔ **Speaker:** Used by the iPhone's built-in speakerphone and plays audio — music or video soundtracks — if no headset is plugged in. It also plays the ringtone you hear when you receive a call.

- ✔ **Lightning connector:** Has two purposes. First, use it to recharge your iPhone's battery by connecting one end of the included cable to the Lightning connector and the other end to the USB power adapter. Second, you can use the Lightning cable to synchronize. Connect one end of the same cable to the Lightning connector and the other end to a USB port on your Mac or PC. (Your iPhone also charges when connected to your computer, but more slowly than when you use the USB power adapter.)

✔ **Microphone:** Lets callers hear your voice when you're not using a headset equipped with a microphone.

 The iPhone 4S, 5, and 5s/c have two microphones. The one on the back is used for FaceTime calls and also works with the main mic (located on the bottom) to suppress unwanted and distracting background sounds on phone calls.

On the sides and front

On the sides and front of your iPhone, you'll find the following (see Figure 1-3):

✔ **Ring/Silent switch:** On the left side of the iPhone — lets you quickly switch between ring mode and silent mode. When the switch is set to ring mode — the up position, with no orange strip — your iPhone plays sounds through the speaker on the bottom. When the switch is set to silent mode — the down position, with an orange strip visible on the switch — your iPhone doesn't make a sound when you receive a call or when an alert pops up. (You can, however, set it to vibrate to alert you of an incoming call or notification.)

 To silence your phone quickly when in ring mode, press the Sleep/Wake button on the top or one of the Volume buttons.

✔ **Volume buttons:** Found just below the Ring/Silent switch. The upper button increases the volume, the lower one decreases it.

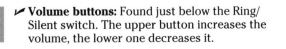

Receiver

Right/Silent switch

Volume buttons

Status bar

App buttons

Touchscreen

Home button

Figure 1-3: The front of the iPhone 5s is a study in elegant simplicity.

- ✔ **SIM card tray:** On the iPhone 4/4S/5/5s/5c, the SIM card tray is on the right side; this is where you remove or replace the SIM card.
- ✔ **Receiver:** The speaker the iPhone uses for telephone calls.
- ✔ **Microphone:** This microphone helps mask ambient noise, and also works with FaceTime calls.
- ✔ **Camera:** The front-facing camera is useful for FaceTime calls.

- ✔ **Touchscreen:** See "Mastering the Multitouch Interface" later in this chapter for more on using the color touchscreen.

- ✔ **Home button:** Press the Home button to display the Home screen. Talk about high-tech: The Home button on the iPhone 5s includes a new fingerprint sensor that can unlock your iPhone when you pass your thumb over it!

- ✔ **App buttons:** Each button on the Home screen launches an included iPhone app or one you've acquired from the App Store.

On the back

On the back of your iPhone is the second camera lens. It's the little circle in the top-left corner. (For more on the camera, see Chapter 5. (Note that this back-facing camera takes better-quality photos than the front-facing camera.) You'll also find the flash to accompany your back-facing camera (which can also be used as a flash-light). And yes, there's yet another microphone (this one well-suited for capturing sound while filming video).

Status bar

The status bar is at the top of the screen and displays tiny icons that provide a variety of information about the current state of your iPhone:

●●●●● **Cell signal:** Tells you whether you're within range of your wireless telephone carrier's cellular network and therefore can make and receive calls. The more solid dots the better, of course.

 Airplane Mode: Indicates that your iPhone is in Airplane Mode, which turns off all wireless features so you can still enjoy music or video during the flight.

LTE **3G/4G/LTE:** Informs you that the high-speed 3G/4G/4G LTE data network from your wireless carrier is available; your iPhone can connect to the Internet via any of these data networks.

GPRS **GPRS:** Indicates that your wireless carrier's GPRS data network is available and that your iPhone can use it to connect to the Internet.

E **EDGE:** Indicates that your wireless carrier's EDGE network is available and you can use it to connect to the Internet.

 Wi-Fi: Indicates that your iPhone is connected to the Internet over a Wi-Fi network. The more bars that are lit in the "fan," the better the connection.

 Network Activity: Indicates that some network activity is occurring, such as over-the-air synchronization, sending or receiving e-mail, or loading a web page.

 VPN: Shows that you are currently connected to a virtual private network (*VPN*).

 Alarm: Tells you that you have set one or more alarms in the Clock application.

Bluetooth: Indicates the current state of your iPhone's Bluetooth connection. Blue indicates that Bluetooth is on and a device is connected. Gray indicates that Bluetooth is on but no device is connected.

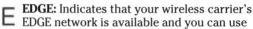 **Battery:** Reflects the level of your battery's charge — completely green when your battery is fully charged or shows a lightning bolt when your iPhone is recharging.

 TTY: Informs you that software support for a teletype (TTY) machine for those who are hearing- or speech-impaired is turned on in General Settings; however, TTY requires an external hardware adapter.

If you've enabled Location Services within the Settings app, your iPhone displays an arrow-shaped pointer to indicate that an app is reading your current location.

Home Sweet Home Screen

Tap the Home button at any time to summon your iPhone's Home screen. If your iPhone is asleep when you press the Home button, the unlock screen appears, where you enter your passcode (or use your thumbprint) to unlock the device. The Home screen offers a bevy of icons, each representing a different built-in app or function.

Three steps let you rearrange icons on your iPhone:

1. **Press and hold any icon until all of the icons begin to "wiggle."**

2. **Drag the icons around until you're happy with their positions.**

3. **Press the Home button to save your arrangement and stop the "wiggling."**

If you haven't rearranged your icons, you see the following applications on your Home screen, starting at the top left (depending on the iOS version you're using, your iPhone may have a different number of icons):

  ✔ **Messages:** Lets you exchange text messages with almost any other cell phone via SMS, as well as MMS. You can also take advantage of *iMessages*, which enable you to send free text, photo, and video messages with Mac computers running OS X Lion, Mountain Lion, and Mavericks (as well as other iOS 5, 6, and iOS 7 devices).

✔ **Calendar:** If you use OS X Calendar, Microsoft Entourage, or Microsoft Outlook as your calendar program on your PC or Mac, you can synchronize events and alerts between your computer and your iPhone. Create an event on one and it automatically syncs with the other the next time they're connected (either wirelessly or by cable).

✔ **Photos:** Indicates the iPhone's terrific photo manager. You can view pictures that you take with the iPhone's built-in camera or transfer photos from your computer.

✔ **Camera:** Lets you shoot a picture with the iPhone's 3-megapixel (iPhone 3GS), 5-megapixel (iPhone 4), or 8-megapixel (iPhone 4S, 5, and 5s/c) camera. Ditto if you want to shoot video on the 3GS, 4, 4S, 5, or 5s/c models — the 4S, 5, and 5s/c can even shoot 1080p HD video!

✔ **Weather:** Monitors the hourly forecast for the next 24 hours, as well as the six-day weather forecast — and not just for your home town, but for as many cities as you like.

✔ **Clock:** Lets you see the current time in as many cities as you like, set one or more alarms, and use your iPhone as a stopwatch or a countdown timer.

✔ **Maps:** Lets you view street maps or satellite images of locations around the globe, ask for directions, check traffic conditions, or find a nearby pizza joint.

✔ **Videos:** Speaking of video, tap this icon to watch movies, TV shows, and music videos.

✔ **Notes:** Lets you type notes that you can save to your iPhone or e-mail to yourself or anyone else.

✔ **Reminders:** Saves your to-do list, complete with visual and audio reminders.

- ✔ **Stocks:** Monitor the performance of your favorite stocks, and catch up on the latest financial news.

- ✔ **Game Center:** Ready to play a game? The Game Center makes it easy to locate friends for a quick challenge or review your achievements.

- ✔ **Newsstand:** If you're familiar with iBooks — Apple's ebook reader — then you'll feel right at home with this periodical and newspaper reader. (It even updates your subscriptions automatically.)

- ✔ **iTunes Store:** Gives you access to the iTunes Store.

- ✔ **App Store:** Enables you to connect to and search the iTunes App Store for iPhone applications you can download.

- ✔ **Passbook:** Stores your airplane boarding passes, event tickets, and store coupons and loyalty cards for easy retrieval.

- ✔ **Compass:** Uses your iPhone's built-In GPS and Wi-Fi to provide an accurate real-time compass, just like your old Scout days.

- ✔ **Settings:** Lets you adjust your iPhone's settings. Mac users, think System Preferences; Windows users, think Control Panel.

- ✔ **Phone:** Tap this application icon to use the iPhone as, well, a phone!

- ✔ **Mail:** This application lets you send and receive e-mail with most e-mail systems.

- ✔ **Safari:** Lets you surf the web with the Safari web browser.

- ✔ **Music:** Unleashes all the power of a video iPod right on your phone.

Now that you and your iPhone have been properly introduced, it's time to begin using it!

Mastering the Multitouch Interface

The iPhone removes the usual physical buttons in favor of a *multitouch display.* It is the heart of many things you do on the iPhone, and the controls change depending on the task at hand.

The iPhone actually includes six keyboard layouts in English, all variations on the alphabetical keyboard, the numeric and punctuation keyboard, and the more punctuation and symbols keyboard. The layout you see on your iPhone depends on the application you are working in. The keyboards in Safari, for example, differ from those in Notes.

The iPhone keyboard contains six keys that don't actually type a character: Shift, Toggle, International keyboard, Dictation, Delete, and Return:

 ✔ **Shift key:** If you're using the alphabetical keyboard, the Shift key switches between uppercase and lowercase letters. If you're using either of the other two keyboards, pressing Shift switches to the one you're not currently using.

 To turn on Caps Lock and type in all caps, you first need to enable Caps Lock. Tap the Settings icon, tap General, and then tap Keyboard. Tap the Enable Caps Lock item to turn it on. After the Caps Lock setting is enabled (it's disabled by default), you double-tap the Shift key to turn on Caps Lock. (The Shift key turns blue when Caps Lock is on.) Tap the Shift key again to turn off Caps Lock. To disable Caps Lock completely, just reverse the process by turning off the Enable Caps Lock setting (tap Settings, General, Keyboard).

- ✔ **Toggle key:** Switches between the different keyboard layouts.

- ✔ **International keyboard key:** Shows up only if you've turned on an international keyboard.

- ✔ **Dictation key:** Toggles dictation mode, where your iPhone types the words you speak.

- ✔ **Delete key:** Erases the character immediately to the left of the cursor.

- ✔ **Return key:** Moves the cursor to the beginning of the next line.

The virtual iPhone keyboard

Here's why this keyboard is so smart:

- ✔ Includes a built-in English dictionary with words from today's popular culture.

- ✔ Adds your contacts to its dictionary automatically.

- ✔ Uses complex analysis algorithms to predict the word you're trying to type.

- ✔ Suggests corrections as you type. It then offers you the suggested word just below the mis-spelled word. When you decline a suggestion and the word you typed is *not* in the iPhone dictionary, the iPhone adds that word to its dictionary and offers it as a suggestion in the future.

 Remember to decline suggestions (by tapping the characters you typed as opposed to the suggested words that appear beneath what you've typed), because doing so helps your intelligent keyboard become even smarter.

- ✔ Reduces the number of mistakes you make as you type by intelligently and dynamically resizing the touch zones for certain keys.

Training your digits

Using the iPhone efficiently means that you need to master a few tricks: Tap, flick, swipe, and pinch:

- ✔ **Tap:** Tapping serves multiple purposes. Tap an icon to open an application from the Home screen, to start playing a song, or to choose the photo album you want to look through. Sometimes, you double-tap (twice in rapid succession) to zoom in (or out) of web pages, maps, and e-mails.

- ✔ **Flick:** A flick of the finger on the screen lets you quickly scroll through lists of songs, e-mails, and picture thumbnails. Tap on the screen to stop scrolling, or merely wait for the scrolling list to stop.

- ✔ **Swipe:** Swipe downward from the top of the screen — all it takes is one finger — and your iPhone displays the Notification Center, where you can track all notifications you've received (including calls and voicemails, messages displayed by apps, and even weather and stock figures). Many apps also allow you to browse photos and screens by swiping left and right across your screen.

- ✔ **Pinch/spread:** Place two fingers on the edges of a web page or picture to enlarge the images or make them smaller. Pinching and spreading are easy to master.

The Home screen discussed earlier in this chapter may not be the only screen of icons on your phone. When you start adding apps from the App Store, you may see two or more tiny dots between the Phone, Mail, Safari, and Music icons and the row of icons directly above them. These dots denote additional screens.

The white dot indicates the screen you're currently viewing. To navigate between screens, either flick from right to left or left to right across the middle of the screen or tap directly on the dots.

The four icons in the last row — Phone, Mail, Safari, and Music — are in a special part of the screen known as the *dock*. When you switch from screen to screen as just described, these icons remain on the screen.

Press the Home button to jump back to the first screen of icons or the Home screen.

 If you press the Home button twice in rapid succession, your iPhone displays the multitasking bar, where the apps that you've used recently (and those that are still running in the background) are conveniently displayed. To close the bar, either tap one of the app icons or press the Home button again.

Finger-typing

If you're patient and trusting, you'll get the hang of finger-typing in a week or so. You have to rely on the virtual keyboard that appears when you tap a text field to enter notes, compose text messages, type the names of new contacts, and so forth.

The keyboard does a pretty good job of coming up with the words you have in mind. As you press your finger against a letter or number on the screen, the individual key you press gets bigger and practically jumps off the screen, as shown in Figure 1-4. That way, you know that you struck the correct letter or number.

Mistakes are common at first. Say that you meant to type a sentence in the Notes application that reads, "I am typing a bunch of notes." But because of the way your fingers struck the virtual keys, you actually entered "I am typing a bunch of *npyrs.*" Fortunately, Apple knows that the *o* you meant to press is next to the *p* that showed up in your text, just as *t* and *y* and the *e* and the *r* are side by side. So the software determines that *notes* was indeed the word you had in mind and places it in red under the suspect word, as shown in Figure 1-5. To accept the suggested word, merely tap the Space key. And if for some reason you actually did mean to type *npyrs* instead, tap on the suggested word (*notes* in this example) to decline it.

When you're typing notes or sending e-mail and want to type a number, symbol, or punctuation mark, tap the 123 key to bring up an alternative virtual keyboard. Tap the ABC key to return to the first keyboard. And when you're in Safari, if you press and hold the .com key, you're offered the choice of .com, .net, .edu, or .org.

Figure 1-4: The ABCs of virtual typing.

You can rotate the iPhone so that its keyboard changes to a wider landscape mode, with slightly larger keys, in most iPhone apps (including Mail, Messages, Notes, Reminders, and Safari).

Don't forget: If you're using an iPhone 4S, 5, or 5s/c, you can eschew the keyboard completely and use your voice to dictate messages, notes, and reminders to *Siri* (the voice assistant). The Dictation key is to the left of the Space key — you can tap it any time you'd normally be typing (like the body of an e-mail message or a text message) and then begin speaking. Tap the Dictation icon to exit Dictation mode.

Figure 1-5: When the keyboard bails you out.

Editing mistakes

It's a good idea to type with reckless abandon and not get hung up over the characters you mistype. Again, the self-correcting keyboard will fix many errors. That said, plenty of typos will likely turn up, especially in the beginning, and you'll have to make corrections manually.

 A neat trick for making corrections is to hold your finger against the screen to bring up the magnifying glass. Use it to position the pointer to the spot where you need to make the correction.

Using Cut, Copy, Paste, and Replace

Being able to copy and paste text (or images) from one place on a computer to another has seemingly been a divine right since Moses. Of course, Apple provides Copy and Paste (and Cut) on the iPhone, as well as another remedy for correcting errors: Replace. (You can also display a definition of the selected word by tapping Define.)

On the iPhone, you might copy text or images from the web and paste them into text, an e-mail, a message, or a note. Or you might copy a bunch of pictures or video into an e-mail.

Here's how to exploit the feature. Let's assume you're jotting down ideas in Notes that you want to copy into an e-mail:

1. **Double-tap a word to select it.**

2. **Drag the blue grab points to expand the highlighted text block. After you select the text, tap Copy. (If you want to delete the text block, tap Cut instead.)**

3. **Open the Mail program and start composing a message.**

4. **Insert the text you just copied into your e-mail message by tapping the cursor. Select, Select All, and Paste commands pop up.**

5. **Tap Paste to paste the text into the message.**

Any time you notice an error in text you've typed or pasted, you can double-tap the word and the options change to Cut, Copy and Paste (and, if you tap the right arrow icon next to Paste, you can choose Replace). Tap Replace and the iPhone serves up a few suggested replacement words. If the word you want to substitute is listed, tap it, and the iPhone automatically makes the switch. If you make a mistake while typing or editing, simply shake the iPhone to undo the last edit.

Organizing with Folders

Finding the single app you want to use among apps spread out across 11 screens is a daunting task. Never fear: Apple includes a handy organization tool called Folders. This feature enables you to create folder icons, each holding up to a dozen apps.

To create a folder, press your finger against an icon until all the icons on the screen jiggle. Decide which apps you want to move to a folder, and drag the icon for the first app on top of the second app. The two apps are now inside a newly created folder. Apple names the folder according to the category of apps inside the folder, but you can easily change the folder name by tapping the X in the bar where the folder name appears and substituting a new name.

To launch an app that's inside a folder, tap that folder's icon and then tap the icon for the app that you want to open. In iOS 7, folders can contain multiple screens, so you'll have plenty of room for your apps. You'll see the familiar white dots that indicate which screen you're displaying within the folder.

You can drag apps into and out of any folder as long as there's room for them.

If you drag all the apps outside the folder, the folder automatically disappears.

Calling on the Control Center

iOS 7 marks the debut of the Control Center, where you can quickly and easily access the controls that most iPhone owners use most often. Swipe upward from the bottom of any screen to display the Control Center, shown in Figure 1-6. (You can even use the upward swipe gesture on the Lock screen, so you don't have to unlock your iPhone to use the Control Center.)

The Control Center enables you to configure the following things:

- ✔ **Wireless connections:** You can quickly turn on or off your Wi-Fi and Bluetooth hardware as needed, or you can toggle Do Not Disturb on and off.

- ✔ **Screen settings:** Choose a new brightness level, or lock your iPhone's display orientation.

- ✔ **Music playback:** Display what track you're playing, pause it, fast-forward or reverse, or adjust the music volume.

- ✔ **AirDrop and AirPlay:** Exchange files with other iOS devices using AirDrop, or stream video to an Apple TV or other devices that support AirPlay.

- ✔ **Apps and functions:** Use your iPhone as a flashlight, display your calculator and countdown timer, or use your iPhone's camera.

Figure 1-6: All your controls in one convenient spot.

Searching with Spotlight

Using the Safari browser, you can search the web via Google, Yahoo!, or Microsoft Bing. But what if you need to search for people and programs across your iPhone?

Searching across the iPhone is based on the Spotlight feature familiar to Mac owners. To access Spotlight, swipe downward from the middle, flick to the left of the main Home screen. or, as mentioned earlier in this chapter, press the Home button from the Home screen. In the bar at the top of the screen that slides into view, enter your search query using the virtual keyboard. The iPhone starts spitting out results the moment you type a single character and the list gets narrowed each time you type an additional character. The results are pretty darn thorough.

Chapter 2

Getting Stuff to and from Your iPhone

• •

In This Chapter

▶ Starting your first sync

▶ Disconnecting during a sync

▶ Syncing all your stuff

• •

*A*fter you understand the basics (see Chapter 1), you probably want to get your stuff (contacts, appointments, events, mail settings, bookmarks, ringtones, music, movies, TV shows, podcasts, audiobooks, photos, and applications) into your iPhone.

The good news is that you can easily copy any or all of those items from your computer to your iPhone. After you do that, you can synchronize your contacts, appointments, and events so they're kept up-to-date automatically in both places — on your computer and your iPhone — whenever you make a change in one place or the other. So when you add or change an appointment, an event, or a contact on your iPhone, that information automatically appears on your computer the next time your iPhone and computer communicate (either using a USB connection or wirelessly).

This communication between your iPhone and computer is called *syncing* (short for synchronizing). Don't worry: It's easy, and we walk you through the entire process in this chapter.

You'll also learn about iCloud, which can automatically transfer data from your iPhone to other iOS 5/6/7 devices and your Mac — and back again. Apple calls this exchange *pushing* (whenever you buy a new song or book on your iPhone, for example, it's wirelessly pushed to your Mac and your iPad through the iCloud).

 The information in this chapter is based on iTunes version 11 and iOS version 7.0, which were the latest and greatest when these words were written. If your screens don't look like ours, upgrade to iTunes 11 and iOS 7.0 (or higher). By the way, they are both free upgrades and offer significant advantages over their predecessors. Go to www.apple.com to upgrade.

Starting to Sync

Synchronizing your iPhone over a cable connection with your computer is a lot like syncing an iPod. If you're an iPod user, the process will be a piece of cake. But it's not too difficult even for those who've never used an iPod or iTunes. (Don't forget, many of the steps in the following process only occur the first time you sync your iPhone — in fact, you may only need to sync using a cable once!)

Follow these steps:

1. **Connect your iPhone to your computer with the USB cable that came with your iPhone.**

   When you connect your iPhone to your computer, iTunes should launch automatically. If it doesn't, you may have plugged the cable into a USB port on your keyboard, monitor, or hub. Try plugging it into one of the USB ports on your computer instead. USB ports on your computer supply more power to a connected device than USB ports on a keyboard, monitor, or most hubs. If iTunes still doesn't launch automatically, try launching it manually.

2. **Select your iPhone in the iTunes source list.**

   You see the Set Up Your iPhone pane. Here you can specify whether you'd like to set up your iPhone as new (starting with all default applications and settings), or whether you'd like to restore from a previous iPhone backup. In this tome, we assume that you're starting a new iPhone.

    If you don't see an iPhone in the source list and you're sure it's connected to a USB port on your computer (not the keyboard, monitor, or hub), restart your computer. If the source list isn't displayed when you connect your iPhone, click View⇨Show Sidebar.

3. **Click the Done button.**

4. **With your iPhone still selected in the source list, click the Summary tab near the top of the window, as shown in Figure 2-1.**

5. **Choose whether you want to back up your iPhone's data to the iCloud or to your computer.**

   By default, your iPhone is set to back up wirelessly using the iCloud Backup feature — if you enable the Automatically Back Up to iCloud radio button on the Summary pane, iTunes does not back up your iPhone data when it's connected by cable. It's easy to specify what data gets backed up to iCloud, but you have to make those choices from your iPhone: tap the Settings icon on the

Home screen and then tap the iCloud item. Turn
on the switch for each type of data you want
backed up. (Remember, however, that your
iPhone must be plugged in to a power source and
must be connected to a Wi-Fi network for an
iCloud Backup.) Tap the Storage & Backup button
and make sure that the iCloud Backup switch is
set to on.

 You can always start an iCloud Backup manually from this same Storage & Backup
screen on your iPhone — tap the Back Up
Now button.

If you'd rather back up using the cable connection, select the Automatically Back Up to This
Computer radio button on the iTunes Summary
pane. If you're security-conscious and want to
password-protect your backups, select the
Encrypt iPhone Backup check box. (If you do
decide to encrypt your backups, click the Change
Password button to enter your own password.)

Summary	Info	Apps	Tones	Music	Movies	TV Shows	Podcasts	iTunes U	Books	Photos

iPhone 5

BatPhone
(16GB) 📶 22%
Capacity: 13.33 GB
Phone Number: +1 (573) 555-5555
Serial Number: C39J55555555

iOS 7.0
Your iPhone software is up to date. iTunes will automatically check
for an update again on 9/29/13.

Check for Update   Restore iPhone...

Backups

Automatically Back Up
⦿ iCloud
Back up the most important data on your iPhone to iCloud.
○ This computer
A full backup of your iPhone will be stored on this computer.
☐ Encrypt iPhone backup
This will also back up account passwords used on this iPhone.
Change Password...

Manually Back Up and Restore
Manually back up your iPhone to this computer or restore a backup
stored on this computer.

Back Up Now   Restore Backup...

Latest Backups:
Yesterday 6:15 AM to iCloud
Yesterday 6:23 AM to this computer

Options

Figure 2-1: The Summary pane is pretty painless.

6. **If you want iTunes to sync your iPhone automatically whenever you connect it to your computer, click to put a check mark in the Automatically Sync When This iPhone Is Connected check box (in the Options area).**

   Don't select this check box if you want to sync manually by clicking the Sync button at the bottom-right corner of the window.

   Your choice in Step 6 is not set in stone. If you select the Automatically Sync When This iPhone Is Connected check box, you can still prevent your iPhone from syncing automatically — after you connect the iPhone to your computer, click the Summary tab in iTunes and uncheck the Automatically Sync When This iPhone Is Connected check box. This prevents iTunes from opening automatically when you connect the iPhone. (You can still start a sync manually.)

7. **To sync automatically with your computer over a Wi-Fi connection, select the Sync with This iPhone over Wi-Fi.**

   Note that enabling this option will still allow your computer to sync with your iPhone when connected with the USB cable. Also, your iPhone must be connected to a power source and **connected** to a Wi-Fi network for Wi-Fi syncing to work.

 You can also configure your iPhone to allow automatic downloads of music, apps, and books that you install on other devices running iOS 5 (or later). Tap the Settings icon on the Home screen and then tap the iTunes & App Store item. Enable each of the media types that you want to automatically receive on your iPhone.

8. **If you want to sync only items that have check marks to the left of their names in your iTunes library, select the Sync Only Checked Songs and Videos check box.**

9. **If you want high-definition videos you import to be automatically converted into smaller standard-definition video files when you transfer them to your iPhone, select the Prefer Standard Definition Videos check box.**

   Standard-definition video files are significantly smaller than high-definition video files. You'll hardly notice the difference when you watch the video on your iPhone but you'll be able to have more video files on your iPhone because they take up less space.

    The conversion from HD to standard definition takes a long time; be prepared for very long sync times when you sync new HD video and have this option enabled.

10. **If you want songs with bit rates higher than 128 kbps converted into smaller-size AAC files when you transfer them to your iPhone, select the Convert Higher Bit Rate Songs to AAC check box.**

    By default, the bit rate is 128 kbps. A higher bit rate means that the song will have better sound quality but use a lot of storage space. Songs that you buy at the iTunes Store or on Amazon.com, for example, have bit rates of around 256 kbps. So, a 4-minute song with a 256-kbps bit rate is around 8MB; convert it to 128-kbps AAC and it will be roughly half that size (that is, around 4MB), while sounding almost as good. Click the pop-up list to specify the bit rate for the target songs.

Most people won't notice much (if any) difference in audio quality when listening to music on most consumer audio gear. So unless you have your iPhone hooked up to a great amplifier and superb speakers or headphones, you probably won't hear much difference. But your iPhone can hold roughly twice as much music if you enable this option. (Oh, and of course your original tracks in iTunes will stay pristine and higher-quality.)

11. **If you want to turn off automatic syncing in the Music and Video panes, select the Manually Manage Music and Videos check box.**

If you decide to uncheck the Open iTunes When This iPhone Is Connected check box, you can always synchronize manually by clicking the Sync button in the bottom-right corner of the window.

By the way, if you've changed any sync settings since the last time you synchronized, the Sync button will instead say Apply.

Disconnecting the iPhone

When the iPhone is syncing with your computer, you see a tiny rotating circular arrow icon in the iPhone status bar (you can still use it normally; just don't unplug it if you're using the cable). After the sync is finished, iTunes displays a message that the iPhone sync is complete and it's okay to disconnect your iPhone.

If you disconnect your iPhone before a sync is completed using the cable, all or part of the sync may fail.

Synchronizing Your Data

Care to customize the syncing process? If so, your
next order of business is to tell iTunes what data you
want to synchronize between your iPhone and your
computer. You do this by clicking the Info tab, which
is to the right of the Summary tab.

The Info pane has five sections: Sync Contacts, Sync
Calendars, Sync Mail Accounts, Other, and Advanced.
The following sections look at them one by one.

iCloud

iCloud is Apple's free service for keeping your iPhone,
iPod touch, iPad, Macs, and PCs synchronized. The
big allure of iCloud is that it can "push" information
such as e-mail, calendars, contacts, and bookmarks
from your computer to and from your iPhone and
keep those items synchronized on your iPhone and
computer(s) wirelessly and without human interven-
tion. Plus, iCloud allows you to re-download apps,
music, and video that you've bought from the iTunes
Store and App Store at any time.

If you're going to use iCloud, you can safely ignore the
information in the "Advanced" section, which deals
with replacing specified information on your iPhone
during a single synchronization.

Sync Contacts

The Contacts section of the Info pane determines how
synchronization is handled for your contacts. One
method is to synchronize all your contacts, as shown
in Figure 2-2. Or you can synchronize any or all
groups of contacts you've created in your computer's
address book program; just select the appropriate

check boxes in the Selected Groups list, and only
those groups will be synchronized.

Figure 2-2: Want to synchronize your contacts? This is where
you set things up.

Note that the section is named Sync Contacts
because Figure 2-2 was captured in iTunes on a
Mac, and the OS X Contacts application is what
it syncs with. If you use a PC, you see a drop-
down menu that gives you the choice of
Outlook, Google Contacts, Windows Address
Book, or Yahoo! Address Book. Don't worry —
the process works the same on either platform.

The iPhone syncs with these address book programs:

- ✔ **Mac:** Contacts, Yahoo! Address Book, or Google
  Contacts
- ✔ **PC:** Outlook, Google Contacts, Windows
  Address Book, or Yahoo! Address Book

On a Mac, you can sync contacts with multiple applications. On a PC, you can sync contacts with only one
application at a time.

If you use Yahoo! Address Book, select the Sync
Yahoo! Address Book Contacts check box, and then
click the Configure button to enter your Yahoo! ID
and password. If you use Google Contacts, select

the Sync Google Contacts check box and then click the Configure button to enter your Google ID and password.

Syncing never deletes a contact from your Yahoo! Address Book if it has a Messenger ID, even if you delete that contact on the iPhone or on your computer.

 To delete a contact that has a Messenger ID, log in to your Yahoo! account with a web browser and delete the contact in your Yahoo! Address Book.

 If you sync with your employer's Microsoft Exchange calendar and contacts, all your personal contacts and calendars will be wiped out.

Sync Calendars

The Sync Calendars section of the Info pane determines how synchronization is handled for your appointments and events. You can synchronize all your calendars, as shown in Figure 2-3. Or you can synchronize any or all individual calendars you've created in your computer's calendar program. Just select the appropriate check boxes.

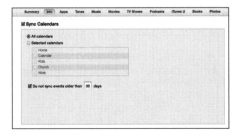

Figure 2-3: Set up syncing for your calendar events here.

The Calendars section in Figure 2-3 is named Sync Calendars because the image was captured in iTunes for the Mac. If you use a PC, this section is named Sync Calendars with Outlook. As before, don't worry — regardless of its name, it works the same on either platform.

The iPhone syncs with the following calendar programs:

- ✔ **Mac:** Calendar, plus any tasks or events that currently sync with Calendar on your Mac
- ✔ **PC:** Microsoft Outlook 2003, 2007, 2010 and 2013

On a Mac, you can sync calendars with multiple applications. On a PC, you can sync calendars with only one application at a time.

One cool thing about syncing your calendar is that if you create reminders, alerts, or alarms in your computer's calendar program, they appear (and sound) on your iPhone at the appropriate date and time, and they also appear in the Notification Center.

Sync Mail Accounts

You can sync account settings for your e-mail accounts in the Sync Mail Accounts section of the Info pane. You can synchronize all your e-mail accounts (if you have more than one), or you can synchronize individual accounts, as shown in Figure 2-4. Just select the appropriate check boxes.

| Summary | Info | Apps | Tones | Music | Movies | TV Shows | Podcasts | iTunes U | Books | Photos |

☑ Sync Mail Accounts

Selected Mail accounts

☑ Gmail
☐ iCloud

Syncing Mail accounts syncs your account settings, but not your messages. To add accounts or make other changes, tap Settings then Mail, Contacts, Calendars on this iPhone.

Figure 2-4: Transfer e-mail account settings to your iPhone here.

The iPhone syncs with the following mail programs:

✔ **Mac:** Mail

✔ **PC:** Microsoft Outlook 2003, 2007, 2010, 2013 and Microsoft Outlook Express

 E-mail account settings are synchronized only one way: from your computer to your iPhone. If you make changes to any e-mail account settings on your iPhone, the changes are *not* synchronized back to the e-mail account on your computer. Trust us: This is a very good feature.

By the way, the password for your e-mail account may or may not be saved on your computer. If you sync an e-mail account and the iPhone asks for a password when you send or receive mail, do this: On the Home screen, tap Settings, Mail, Contacts, Calendars. Tap your e-mail account's name, tap it again on the following screen, and then type your password in the appropriate field.

Other

The settings available in the Other section of the Info pane vary depending on whether you're syncing over Wi-Fi using iCloud or syncing over a cable connection.

If you're syncing using iCloud, there are actually no settings to make in this section. If you're syncing over cable, however, you can select the Sync Safari Bookmarks check box if you want to sync the bookmarks on your computer with bookmarks on your iPhone. The iPhone can sync bookmarks with the following web browsers:

- ✔ **Mac:** Safari
- ✔ **PC:** Microsoft Internet Explorer and Firefox

Advanced

Every so often the contacts, calendars and mail accounts on your iPhone get so screwed up that the easiest way to fix things is to erase that information on your iPhone and replace it with information from your computer (either wirelessly or over the cable connection). If that happens, just click to select the appropriate check boxes in the Advanced section of the Info tab, as shown in Figure 2-5. Then the next time you sync, that information on your iPhone is replaced with information from your computer.

Advanced

Replace information on this iPhone
- ☑ Contacts
- ☑ Calendars
- ☑ Mail Accounts
  Bookmarks

During the next sync only, iTunes will replace the selected information on this iPhone with information from this computer.

Figure 2-5: Replace the information on your iPhone with the information on your computer.

Because the Advanced section is at the bottom of the Info pane and you have to scroll down to see it, it's easy to forget that it's there. Although you probably won't need this feature very often (if ever), you'll be happy it's there if you need it.

Synchronizing Your Media

If you choose to let iTunes manage synchronizing your data automatically — either by cable or wirelessly — this section looks at how you get your media (that's your ringtones, music, podcasts, video, photos and more) from your computer to your iPhone.

 Ringtones, music, podcasts, and video (but not photos) are synced only one way: from your computer to your iPhone. Deleting any of these items from your iPhone does not delete them from your computer when you sync. The only exceptions are songs, ringtones, podcasts, video, and applications that you purchase or download with the iTunes or App Store apps on your iPhone. Such items are, as you'd expect, copied to your computer automatically when you sync. (You can also re-download digital media to your iPhone that you've bought through the iTunes Store at any time — iCloud keeps track of everything you've purchased.)

If you take photos or video using your iPhone's camera — or if you save pictures from e-mail messages and web pages (by pressing and holding on an image and then tapping the Save Image button) or screen shots (which can be created by pressing the Home and Sleep/Wake buttons simultaneously) — these too can be synced.

Ringtones, music, podcasts, movies, TV shows, books, and iTunes U

You use the Tones, Music, Podcasts, Movies, TV Shows, Books, and iTunes U panes to specify the media you want to copy from your computer to your iPhone. To view any of these panes, make sure that your iPhone is still selected in the source list and click the appropriate tab near the top of the window.

Note that some panes won't appear unless you've added that type of media to your library — for example, iTunes U doesn't appear unless you've added something from iTunes U to your iTunes library.

Ringtones

If you have any custom ringtones in your iTunes library, select the Sync Tones check box in the Tones pane. Then you can choose either all ringtones or choose individual ringtones by selecting their check boxes.

Music, music videos, and voice memos

To transfer music to your iPhone, select the Sync Music check box in the Music pane. You can then select the button for Entire Music Library or Selected Playlists, Artists, Albums, and Genres. If you choose the latter, click the check boxes next to particular playlists, artists, and genres you want to transfer. You also can choose to include music videos or voice memos or both by selecting the appropriate check boxes at the top of the pane (see Figure 2-6). Finally, if you select the Automatically Fill Free Space with Songs check box, iTunes fills any free space on your iPhone with music.

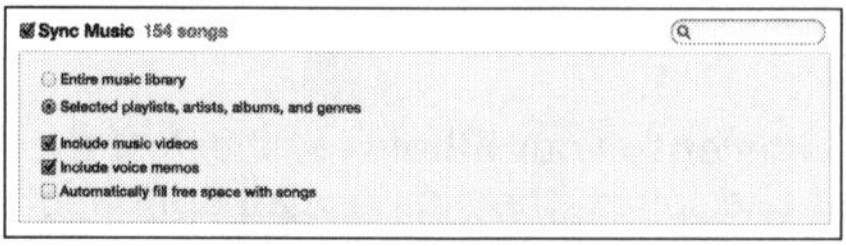

Figure 2-6: Use the Music pane to copy music, music videos, and voice notes from your computer to your iPhone.

If you choose Entire Music Library and have more songs in your iTunes library than storage space on your iPhone — more than about 15GB on a 16GB, 31GB on a 32GB iPhone, or 63GB on 64GB iPhone — you see an error message complaining that iTunes can't sync because there isn't enough room.

To avoid these errors, select playlists, artists, and genres that total less than 15, 31, or 63 gigabytes.

 Music, podcasts, and video are notorious for chewing up massive amounts of storage space on your iPhone. If you try to sync too much media, you'll see lots of error messages. Forewarned is forearmed.

Podcasts

To transfer podcasts to your iPhone, select the Sync Podcasts check box in the Podcasts pane. Then you can choose All Podcasts or Selected Podcasts.

Regardless of whether you choose to sync all podcasts or only selected podcasts, a pop-up menu enables you to specify which episodes you want to sync.

If you have episodes of podcasts on your playlists, you can include them by selecting the appropriate check box under Include Episodes from Playlists.

Movies

To transfer movies to your iPhone, first select the Sync Movies check box, then choose an option for movies you want to include automatically from the pop-up menu as shown in Figure 2-7. If you choose an

option other than All (we've selected 3 Most Recent)
you can optionally select individual movies and playlists
by checking the boxes in appropriate sections.

Figure 2-7: Your choices in the Movies pane determine which
movies are copied to your iPhone.

TV Shows

The procedure for syncing TV shows is slightly different from the procedure for syncing movies. First,
select the Sync TV Shows check box to enable TV
show syncing. Then choose how many episodes to
include and whether you want all shows or only
selected shows from the two pop-up menus, as shown
in Figure 2-8.

If you want to also include individual episodes or episodes on playlists, select the appropriate check boxes
in the Shows, Episodes (*South Park* Episodes in
Figure 2-8) and Include Episodes from Playlists sections of the TV Shows pane.

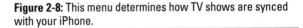

Figure 2-8: This menu determines how TV shows are synced with your iPhone.

iTunes U

To sync educational content from iTunes U (a part of the iTunes Store that offers lectures, audiobooks, language lessons, and so on), first select the Sync iTunes U check box to enable iTunes U syncing. Then choose how many episodes to include and whether you want all collections or only selected collections from the two pop-up menus.

If you want to also include individual items or items on playlists, select the appropriate check boxes in the Items section and Include Items from Playlists section of the iTunes U pane.

Books

To sync electronic books and audiobooks from the iTunes Store, first select the Sync Books check box to enable book syncing. Then choose whether to sync all books or only selected books.

Note that audiobooks have their own Sync check box on this pane — and again, you can choose between syncing all of your audiobooks or just those you select.

Photos

Syncing photos is a little different from syncing other media because your iPhone has a built-in camera — two cameras, actually, on the iPhone 4/4S/5/5s — and you may want to copy pictures you take with the iPhone to your computer, as well as copy pictures stored on your computer to your iPhone.

The iPhone syncs photos with these programs:

- ✔ **Mac:** Aperture or iPhoto
- ✔ **PC:** Adobe Photoshop Album or Adobe Photoshop Elements

You can also sync photos with any folder on your computer that contains images.

To sync photos, click the Photos tab at the top of the window. In the Photos pane, select the Sync Photos From check box, and then choose an application or folder from the pop-up menu (iPhoto in Figure 2-9).

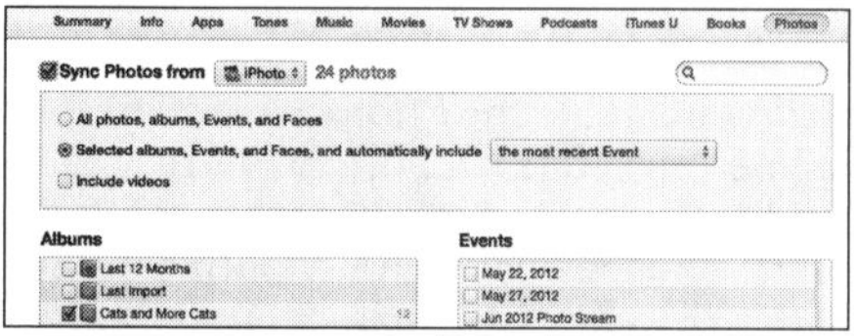

Figure 2-9: The Photos pane determines which photos will be synchronized with your iPhone.

If you choose an application that supports photo albums, events, and/or facial recognition, as we have in Figure 2-9 by choosing iPhoto, you can automatically include events by making a selection from the pop-up menu or select specific albums, events, and/or faces to sync by selecting individual albums, events, or faces in the areas below. If you are using iPhoto, you can also type a word or phrase into the search field at the top-right corner of the iTunes window to search for specific events.

If you choose a folder full of images, you can create subfolders inside it that will appear as albums on your iPhone. But if you choose an application that doesn't support albums or events, or a single folder full of images with no subfolders, you have to transfer all or nothing.

Because we selected iPhoto in the Sync Photos From menu, and iPhoto supports events and faces in addition to albums, we also have the option of syncing events, faces, or both if we prefer.

If you've taken any photos with your iPhone since the last time you synced it, the appropriate program launches (or the appropriate folder is selected), and you have the option of downloading the pictures to your computer. The process is the same as when you download pictures from your digital camera.

Your iPhone can also automatically sync new photos with iPhoto if you enable the Photo Stream option in Settings (tap Settings, tap iCloud, tap Photos, and then turn on My Photo Stream). Because we're talking iCloud here, this syncing is naturally both wireless and automatic! You can also create Shared Photo Streams within iPhoto, which enable you to send photos to specific contacts and groups.

Applications

If you have downloaded or purchased any iPhone applications from the iTunes App Store, click the Apps tab. Now choose the individual applications you want to transfer to your iPhone by selecting their check boxes from the list.

You can sort your applications by name, category, kind, size, or date acquired. Or you can type a word or phrase into the search field (at the top-right corner of the iTunes window) to search for a specific application.

Finally, you can rearrange application icons in iTunes by dragging them where you want them to appear on your iPhone. The next time you sync, the apps on your phone will be rearranged just the way you arranged them in iTunes. If you have a lot of apps, you're sure to love this feature.

How much space did I use?

If you're interested in knowing how much free space is available on your iPhone, look near the bottom of the iTunes window while your iPhone is selected in the source list. You see a chart that shows the contents of your iPhone, color-coded for your convenience. (See Figure 2-10.)

Figure 2-10: This handy chart shows you how much space is being used on your iPhone.

 Here's a cool trick: Hover your cursor over any of the sections in the chart, and you see specifics on just how many items are included in that section and how much space they take up on your iPhone.

In case you're wondering, Other is the catchall category for contacts, calendars, appointments, events, bookmarks, notes, and e-mail stored on your phone. In our case, the total of these items is over a gigabyte, a fraction of the total storage space available on this iPhone.

Chapter 3

Making Calls and Sending Messages

· ·

In This Chapter

▶ Making a call

▶ Visualizing visual voicemail

▶ Recording a greeting

▶ Using Siri and Voice Control

▶ Receiving a call

▶ Sending and receiving SMS/MMS/iMessage messages

▶ Video chatting with FaceTime

· ·

*T*he iPhone's most critical mission is the one from which its name is derived — it is first and foremost a cell phone. Aside from making it easy for you to make regular phone calls, the iPhone makes sending text messages simple and fun.

This chapter is devoted to the nifty ways you can handle wireless calls on an iPhone and keep in touch with text messages. We focus on the three types of iPhone message protocols: SMS, MMS, and iMessage.

Making a Call

To make a call, start by tapping the Phone icon on the Home screen. You can then make calls by tapping any of the icons that show up at the bottom of the screen: Contacts, Favorites, Recents, Keypad, or Voicemail. Owners of iPhone 3GS and iPhone 4 models can dial a phone number or a particular person by voice, while owners of an iPhone 4S, 5, or 5s/c can also use Siri, the voice assistant. Let's take these options one by one.

Contacts

You can get your snail-mail addresses, e-mail addresses, and (most relevant for this chapter) phone numbers that reside on your PC or Mac into the iPhone by syncing or via iCloud (see Chapter 2 if you need help with this task). Assuming that you've already mastered that task, all those addresses and phone numbers are now hanging out in one place. Their not-so-secret hiding place is revealed when you tap the Contacts icon inside the Phone application or the Contacts icon within the Utilities folder (by default, found on the second screen page).

Here's how to make those contacts work for you:

1. **Inside the Phone application, tap Contacts.**

2. **Flick your finger so the list of contacts on the screen scrolls rapidly up or down.**

   Alternatively, you can move your fingers along the alphabet on the right edge of the Contacts list or tap one of the tiny letters to jump to names that begin with that letter.

   You also can find a list of potential matches by starting to type the name of a contact in the search field near the top of the list. Or type the

name of the place where your contact works.
You may have to flick to get the search field into
view. You can also find people using Spotlight
search (see Chapter 1).

3. **When you're at or near the appropriate contact**
   name, stop the scrolling by tapping the screen.

 Note that when you tap to stop the scrolling,
that tap doesn't select an item in the list. That
may seem counterintuitive the first few times
you try it.

Double-tap the status bar (which reads All
Contacts) to automatically scroll to the top of
the list. This is useful if you're really popular
and have a whole bunch of names among your
contacts.

4. **Tap the name of the person you want to call.**

   As shown in Figure 3-1, you can see a bunch of
   fields with the individual's phone numbers, physical and e-mail addresses, FaceTime information,
   and possibly even a mug shot. Odds are pretty
   good that the person has more than one phone
   number, so the hardest decision you must make
   is choosing which of these to call.

5. **Tap the phone icon next to the desired number,**
   and the iPhone initiates the call.

If you lumped your contacts into Groups on your
computer, reflecting, say, different departments in
your company or friends from work, friends from
school, and so on, you can tap the Groups button
on the upper-left side of the All Contacts screen to
access these groups.

 Your own iPhone phone number, lest you forget
it, appears at the top of the Contacts list, if you
arrived in Contacts from the Phone application.

Figure 3-1: We figured this contact would be here.

Favorites

Consider Favorites the iPhone equivalent of speed-dialing. It's where you can keep a list of the people and numbers you dial most often. Merely tap the person's name in Favorites to call that person.

You can set up as many favorites as you need for a person. For example, you can create separate Favorites listings for your spouse's office phone number, FaceTime number, and cell number.

Setting up favorites is a breeze. When looking at one of your contacts, you may have noticed the Add to

Favorites button. When you tap this button, all the phone numbers you have for that person pop up. Tap the number you want to make into a favorite and it turns up on the list. (Note that iPhone 4/4S/5/5s owners can also specify a number as a FaceTime favorite, either as a full FaceTime video call or a FaceTime audio-only call.)

 You can rearrange the order in which your favorites are displayed. To do so, tap Edit; then, to the right of the person you want to move, press your finger against the symbol that looks like three short horizontal lines stacked on top of one another. Drag that symbol to the place on the list where you want your favorite contact to appear.

You can designate new favorites from within the Favorites screen by tapping the + symbol at the upper-right corner of the screen. Doing so brings you back to Contacts. From there, choose the appropriate person and number. A star appears next to any contact's number picked as a favorite.

If any of your chosen folks happens to fall out of favor, you can easily kick them off the Favorites roster. Here's how:

1. **Tap the Edit button in the upper-left corner of the screen.**

   A red circle with a horizontal white line appears to the left of each name in the list.

2. **Tap the circle next to the A-lister getting the heave-ho.**

   A red Delete button appears to the right of the name, as shown in Figure 3-2.

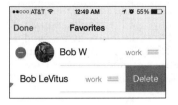

Figure 3-2: I don't like you as much anymore.

3. **Tap Delete.**

   The person (or one of his or her given phone numbers) is no longer afforded the privilege of being in your iPhone inner circle.

Booting someone off the Favorites list does not remove that person from the main Contacts list. After all, the scoundrel may return to your good graces.

Recents

Tapping the Recents icon displays the iPhone call log. The Recents feature houses logs of all recent calls made or received, as well as calls that you missed. Tap All to show all the recent calls and Missed to show just those you missed. Under the All list, completed calls and missed calls that have been returned by clicking the red entry are shown in black; missed calls that haven't been returned in this fashion are shown in red. You also see a descriptor for the phone you were calling or from which you received a call (home, mobile, and so on).

By tapping the small blue circle with the lowercase "i" next to an item in the list (which we call the Info Icon), you can access information about the time a call was made or missed, as well as any known information about the caller from your Contacts information.

To return a call, just tap anywhere on the name.

 If one of the calls you missed came from some- one who isn't already in your Contacts, you can add him or her. Tap the Info icon, and then tap the Create New Contact button.

If the person is among your Contacts but has a new number, tap the Add to Existing Contact button. When the list gets too long, tap Edit and then tap Clear to clean it up.

Keypad

From time to time, of course, you have to dial the number of a person or company who hasn't earned a spot in your Contacts.

That's when you want to tap the keypad icon to bring up the large keys on the virtual touch-tone keypad you see in Figure 3-3. It's surprisingly simple to manu- ally dial a number on this keypad. Just tap the appro- priate keys and tap Call.

 To add this number to your address book, tap the Add to Contacts button that appears under the number.

Visual voicemail

How often have you had to listen to four or five voice- mail messages before getting to the message you want to hear? As shown in Figure 3-4, the iPhone's clever visual voicemail presents a list of your voice- mail messages in the order received. But you need not listen to those messages in that order.

Figure 3-3: A virtually familiar way to dial.

How do you even know you have voicemail?

- ✔ A red circle showing the number of pending messages awaiting your attention appears above the Phone icon on the Home screen or above the Voicemail icon from within the Phone application.

- ✔ You may also see a notification on the iPhone display that says something like, "New voice-mail from Ed." You can configure these notifica-tions from the Notifications item within the Settings app.

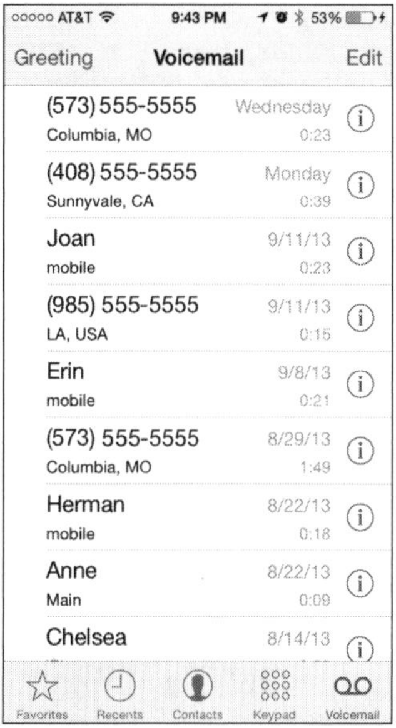

Figure 3-4: Visual voicemail in action.

Whatever draws you in, tap the Voicemail icon to display the list of voicemails. You see the caller's phone
number, assuming this info is known via CallerID, and
in some cases, his or her name. Or you see the word
Unknown.

The beauty of all this, of course, is that you can
ignore (or at least put off listening to) certain
messages.

A blue dot next to a name or number signifies that
you haven't heard the message yet.

To play back a voicemail, tap the name or number in question. Tap the Pause icon to pause the message; tap again to resume. Tap the Speaker button if you want to hear the message through the iPhone's speakerphone. To replay the message again, tap the Play button.

 Tap the blue Info icon next to a caller's name or number to bring up any contact info on the person or to add the caller to your Contacts.

 The tiny playhead along the Scrubber bar shows you the length of the message and how much of the message you've heard. When callers ramble on forever, you can drag the playhead to rapidly advance through a message. Perhaps more importantly, if you miss something, you can replay that segment.

Returning a call is as simple as tapping the Call Back button. And you can delete a voicemail by tapping Delete.

If you have no phone service, you see a message that says _Visual Voicemail is currently unavailable._

 You can listen to your iPhone voicemail from another phone. Just dial your iPhone number and, while the greeting plays, enter your voicemail password. You can set up such a password by tapping Settings from the Home screen and then tapping Phone. Tap Change Voicemail Password. You're asked to enter your current voicemail password if you already have one. Type it and tap Done. If you haven't set up a password previously, tap Done. You're asked to type a new password; then you tap Done twice.

Recording a greeting

You have two choices when it comes to your voice-mail greeting. You can accept a generic greeting with your phone number by default. Or you can create a custom greeting in your own voice by following these steps:

1. **Inside the voicemail application, tap the Greeting button.**

2. **Tap Custom.**

3. **Tap Record and start dictating a clever, deserving-of-being-on-the-iPhone voicemail greeting.**

4. **When you have finished recording, tap Stop.**

5. **Review the greeting by pressing Play.**

6. **If the greeting is worthy, tap Save. If not, tap Cancel and start over at Step 1.**

Voice dialing

If you have an iPhone 3GS or 4, you can make a call by simply opening your mouth. To summon Voice Control, press and hold the Home button or press and hold the center button on the wired headset with the remote and microphone supplied with the iPhone.

Wait for the tone and speak clearly, especially if you're in a noisy environment. You can dial by number, as in "Dial 202-555-1212." You can dial a name, as in "Call Bob LeVitus" or "Dial Ed Baig." Or you can be a tad more specific as in "Dial Bob LeVitus mobile" or "Call Ed Baig home." Before the number is dialed, an automated female voice repeats what she thinks she heard.

If the person you're calling has multiple phone numbers and you fail to specify which one, the female voice prompts you, "Ed Baig, home, mobile, or work?" Tell her which one it is, or say "Cancel" if you decide not to call.

 When the Voice Control screen appears, let go of the Home button before speaking a command. Otherwise, your thumb may cover the microphone, making it more difficult for the iPhone to understand your intent.

Conversing with Siri

Owners of the iPhone 4S, 5. and 5s/c can call upon *Siri*, the iPhone voice assistant, which provides you with enhanced control over all sorts of iPhone tasks. (Think "Voice Control" after your iPhone has undergone a *serious* college education.)

 Siri requires a Wi-Fi or 3G/4G/LTE connection to the Internet.

You activate Siri in the same way as Voice Control on older iPhones. Press and hold the Home button — after you hear the tone, you can issue a command or ask Siri, "What can you do?" (Take our word for it — the response you'll get is a real eye-opener!) Again, the quieter the environment, the better.

Unlike Voice Control, Siri's capabilities extend far beyond just voice dialing and playing music. You can control virtually all of the important apps on your iPhone — and you can launch many apps directly by simply saying "Launch" followed by the app name (such as "Launch Music"). For example, try out these commands:

- ✔ **Safari:** "Search the Web for…"
- ✔ **Weather:** "Tell me the weather."
- ✔ **Maps:** "How do I get to…"

✓ **FaceTime:** "FaceTime Bob"

✓ **Messages:** "Tell my Dad…"

✓ **Notes:** "Note that…"

✓ **Calendar:** "Make an appointment…"

Siri is intelligent enough to recognize different verbs for the same action, like "Tell Bob to sell 20 shares" or "Send a message to Bob saying sell 20 shares." (Are you starting to feel like George Jetson right about now?)

Like Voice Control, Siri also audibly confirms your command — but she also displays your command on the screen and the response she wants to make. Siri also displays a thumbnail for the corresponding app, along with related information (for example, the text of an e-mail message you've asked Siri to read or an event in Calendar you've asked her to add). You can tap this information display to launch the app directly.

While Siri is active, you can issue another command or clarify your request by tapping the microphone icon at the bottom of the screen. (Like any good assistant, Siri allows you to add, cancel, or change information before acting on your command.)

Receiving a Call

It's wonderful to have numerous options for making a call. But what are your choices when somebody calls you? The answer depends on whether you are willing to take the call. Luckily, the iPhone includes caller ID display for those numbers in your Contacts list.

Accepting the call

To accept a call, you have several options:

✔ Tap Answer and greet the caller in whatever language makes sense.

✔ If the phone is locked, drag the Answer slider to the right.

✔ Swipe up and Tap the Respond with Text button to send a text message or iMessage to the caller.

✔ Tap the Remind Me Later to display a reminder to call the person back.

✔ If you are donning the stereo earbuds that come with the iPhone, click the microphone button.

If you are listening to music in your iPhone's iPod when a call comes in, the song stops playing and you have to decide whether to take the call. If you do, the music resumes from where you left off when the conversation ends.

Rejecting the call

We're going to assume that you're not a cold-hearted person out to break a caller's heart. Rather, we assume that you are a busy person who will call back at a more convenient time. Keeping that positive spin in mind, here are three ways to reject a call on the spot and send the call to voicemail:

✔ **Tap Decline.** Couldn't be easier than that.

✔ **Press the Sleep/Wake button twice in rapid succession.** (The button is on the top of the device.)

✔ **Using the supplied headset, press and hold the Microphone button for a couple of seconds and then let go.** Two beeps let you know that the call was indeed rejected.

Sometimes you're perfectly willing to take a call, but you need to silence the ringer or turn off the vibration. To do so, press the Sleep/Wake button a single time, or press one of the volume buttons. You'll still have the opportunity to answer.

iOS 7 also features *Do Not Disturb*, which you can configure within Settings. When you turn on Do Not Disturb within Settings (or from the Control Center), all alerts and ringtones are turned off. (You can also specify just a handful of contacts that can reach you no matter what.)

Messaging

The Messages application lets you exchange short text messages with any cell phone that supports the SMS protocol. Your iPhone also supports the MMS protocol, which lets you also exchange pictures, contacts, videos, ringtones (and other audio recordings) with any cell phone that supports the MMS protocol. Finally, if you're using any iPhone that's running iOS 5 or later, you can send iMessages with text, video, or audio — free of charge — to any other device running iOS 5 or later. (The list includes another iPhone, an iPad, or an iPod touch, as well as a Mac running OS X Lion or later.)

SMS is the acronym for the Short Message Service protocol; MMS is the acronym for the Multimedia Messaging Service protocol. Most mobile phones sold today support one or both protocols.

MMS support is built into iPhone OS 3.0 and higher and works with iPhone 3G/3GS and 4/4S/5/5s (but not the first-generation iPhone).

Typing text on a cell phone with a 12-key numeric keypad is an unnatural act, which is why many cell phone users have never sent a single SMS or MMS message. The iPhone changes that. The intelligent virtual keyboard makes it easy to compose short text messages, and the big, bright, high-resolution screen makes it a pleasure to read them. (On an iPhone 4S, 5, or 5s/c, you can even command Siri to create a text message for you using only your voice!)

But before we get to the part where you send or receive a message, let's go over some basics for SMS/MMS:

- ✔ **Both sender and receiver need SMS- or MMS-enabled mobile phones.** Your iPhone qualifies, as does almost any mobile phone made in the past four or five years. Keep in mind that if you send messages to folks with phones that don't support SMS or MMS — or to folks who choose not to pay extra for messaging services — they will never get your message, nor will they even know you sent a message.

- ✔ **Some phones (not the iPhone, of course) limit SMS messages to 160 characters.** If you try to send a longer message to one of these phones, your message may be cut off or split into multiple shorter messages. The point is that it's a good idea to keep SMS messages brief.

- ✔ **Most iPhone plans no longer include free SMS or MMS messages.** You'll be billed for individual SMS or MMS text messages unless you subscribe to the unlimited texting plan. Note that MMS is available from AT&T at no additional cost to customers with an SMS text-messaging bundle.

Each individual message in a conversation counts against this total, even if it's only a one-word reply such as "OK" or "CUL8R" (which is text-speak for "see you later").

- ✔ **You can usually increase the number of messages in your plan for a few more dollars a month.** This is almost always less expensive than paying for them à la carte.

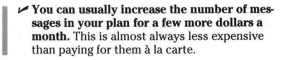

✔ **You can send or receive messages only over
your wireless carrier's network (AT&T, Sprint,
or Verizon in the U.S.).** In other words, SMS and
MMS messages can't be sent or received over a
Wi-Fi connection — however, iMessage works
fine over both Wi-Fi and cellular connections.

Okay, now that we have that out of the way, let's start
with how to send messages.

Sending an SMS message

Tap the Messages icon on the Home screen to
launch the Messages application (known as
Text on earlier versions of the iPhone software), and then tap the little pencil-and-paper
icon in the top-right corner of the screen to
start a new text message.

The To field is active and awaiting your input. You
can do three things at this point:

✔ If the recipient isn't in your Contacts list, type
his or her cell-phone number.

✔ If the recipient *is* in your Contacts list, type the
first few letters of the name. A list of matching
contacts appears. Scroll through it if necessary
and tap the name of the contact.

The more letters you type, the shorter the list
becomes.

✔ Tap the blue plus icon on the right side of the To
field to select a name from your Contacts list.

There's a fourth option if you want to compose the
message first and address it later. Tap inside the text-
entry field (the oval-shaped area just above the keyboard and to the left of the Send button) to activate it
and then type your message. When you've finished

typing, tap the To field and use one of the preceding techniques to address your message.

When you have finished addressing and composing, tap the Send button to send your message on its merry way. That's all there is to it.

Receiving an SMS message

First things first. If you want an alert to sound when you receive a message, tap the Settings icon on your Home screen, tap Sounds, tap the Text Tone item, and then tap one of the available sounds. You can audition the sounds by tapping them.

You hear the sounds when you audition them in the Settings app, even if you have the Ring/Silent switch set to Silent. After you exit the Settings application, however, you *won't* hear a sound when a message arrives if the Ring/Silent switch is set to Silent, or if you've turned on the Do Not Disturb feature. (Your iPhone still displays a notification, however.)

If you *don't* want to hear an alert when a message arrives, instead of tapping one of the listed sounds, tap the first item in the list: None.

If you receive a message when your phone is asleep, all or part of the text message and the name of the sender appear on the Unlock screen when you wake your phone.

If your phone is awake and unlocked when a message arrives, all or part of the message and the name of the sender appear at the top of the screen (as well as in the Notification Center, which you can display by swiping downward from the top of the screen). At the same time, the Messages icon on the Home screen displays the number of unread messages.

You can, however, set your iPhone to display an alert (which enables you to reply immediately.) Tap Settings, tap Notification Center, and then tap the Messages entry and choose the Alerts setting. Now you can read or reply to a text message by tapping Reply when the message appears.

If you're not using alerts, tap the Messages icon to read or reply to a message. If a message other than the one you're interested in appears on the screen when you launch the Messages application, tap Messages in the top-left corner of the screen, and then tap the recipient's name; that person's messages appear on the screen.

To reply to the message on the screen, tap the text-entry field to the left of the Send button, and the keyboard appears. Type your reply and then tap Send.

 Tap the Dictation key — the key to the left of Space, which bears a microphone symbol — and you can dictate text directly into the text-entry field!

Your conversation is saved as a series of text bubbles. Your messages appear on the right side of the screen in blue bubbles; the other person's messages appear on the left in gray bubbles, as shown in Figure 3-5.

What they said   What you said

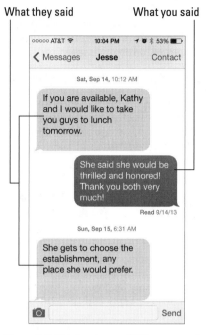

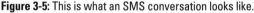

Figure 3-5: This is what an SMS conversation looks like.

You can delete a conversation in two ways:

- ✔ **If you're viewing the conversation:** Tap and hold your finger on any message in the conversation to see a number of circles appear to the left of each message. Now you can delete the entire conversation in one fell swoop by tapping the Delete All button in the top-left corner of the screen.

> ✔ **If you're viewing the list of text messages:**
> Tap the Edit button at the top left of the Text
> Messages list, tap the red minus icon that
> appears to the left of the person's name, and
> then tap the Delete button that appears to the
> right of the name.

MMS: Like SMS with media

To send a picture or video (iPhone 3GS, 4/4S, or 5
only) in a message, follow the instructions for sending
a text message and then tap the camera icon to the
left of the text-entry field at the bottom of the screen.
You then have the option of using an existing picture
or video or taking a new one. You can also add text to
photos or videos if you like. When you're finished, tap
the Send button.

If you *receive* a picture or video in a message, it
appears in a bubble just like text. Tap it to see it
full-screen.

Tap the icon in the lower-left corner (the one
that looks like an arrow trying to escape from a
rectangle) for additional options. If you don't
see the icon, tap the picture or video once and
the icon magically appears.

iMessage: iOS 5/6/7 messaging

Although the party is limited to owners of iOS 5/6/7
devices, iMessage provides everything that MMS
includes — video, locations, contacts, and photos —
and iMessages can be sent over a Wi-Fi connection as
well as a cellular connection. Plus, they're as free as
the air around you!

iMessage operates just like MMS. To verify that you're
using iMessage, check the information line at the top
of a conversation — it should read *iMessage*.

Smart messaging tricks

Here are some more things you can do with messages:

- ✔ To send a message to someone in your Favorites or Recents list, tap the Phone icon on the Home screen, and then tap Favorites or Recents, respectively. Tap the blue Info icon to the right of a name or number, and then tap the Send Message icon (which looks like a Message bubble).

- ✔ To call or e-mail someone to whom you've sent an SMS or MMS message, tap the Messages icon on the Home screen, and then tap the person's name in the Messages list. Tap the Contact button at the top of the conversation and then tap the Phone, FaceTime, or Mail icon to call, FaceTime, or send an e-mail to the person.

 You can use this technique only if the contact has the corresponding information (like a FaceTime number or an e-mail address).

- ✔ To add someone to whom you've sent an SMS or MMS message to your Contacts list, tap the person's name or phone number in the Messages list and then tap the Contact button. Tap the Info icon that appears and then tap Create New Contact.

- ✔ If a message includes a URL, tap it to open that web page in Safari.

- ✔ If a message includes a phone number, tap it to call that number.

- ✔ If a message includes an e-mail address, tap it to open a pre-addressed e-mail message in Mail.

- ✔ If a message includes a street address, tap it to see a map in Maps.

And that's all there is to it. You are now an official messaging maven.

Seeing Is Believing with FaceTime

Using FaceTime video calling is as easy as making a regular call on the iPhone. Plus, FaceTime comes with at least two major benefits *besides* the video factor:

- ✔ FaceTime calls don't count against your regular carrier minutes.
- ✔ The audio quality on FaceTime calls is superior to a regular cell phone connection.

But FaceTime also has a couple of major caveats:

- ✔ Both you and the party you're talking to must have an iPhone 4 or later, a Mac (running OS X Snow Leopard or later), or an iOS device compatible with FaceTime (like an iPad 2/3 or iPod touch). FaceTime doesn't work with older models of the iPhone.
- ✔ Both you and the caller at the other end must be accessing either Wi-Fi or a 3G/4G/LTE cellular connection. The quality of the experience depends on a solid connection.

If you meet the requirements, here's how to make FaceTime happen:

1. **The first time you make a FaceTime call, dial the person's regular iPhone number using any of the methods described earlier.**

2. **Once a regular call is established and you've broached the subject of going to video, tap the FaceTime button.**

   A few seconds later, the other person gets the option to decline or answer the FaceTime invitation by tapping the red button or the green button, respectively. If the person answers, you need to wait a few seconds before you can see the other person. In the same fashion as receiving a voice call, iOS 7 also allows you to decline the FaceTime call with a reminder to return the call, or decline the call and reply instead with a text message.

If you want to mute a FaceTime call, tap the microphone icon with the slash running through it. The caller is still connected, but he cannot hear you. To hide the Mute, Switch Camera, and End buttons, just tap any part of the image.

Chapter 4

Playing Music and Videos

* * *

In This Chapter

▶ Using the built-in iPod

▶ Managing your tunes

▶ Finding videos to watch

* * *

*B*esides being a super-cool phone, your iPhone is also one heck of an iPod. In this chapter, we show you how to use your iPhone to play both audio and video.

Apple doesn't supply the iTunes software in the box with the iPhone, so make sure you have downloaded the latest version of iTunes to your PC or Mac. Just head to www.apple.com/itunes if you need to fetch a copy, or launch your current version of iTunes and then choose Check for Updates. You can find it under the Help menu on a Windows machine and on the iTunes menu on a Mac.

For the rest of this chapter, we assume that you've downloaded iTunes and synced your iPhone with your computer (see Chapter 2 if you need help with that task) and that your iPhone contains audio content — songs or audiobooks. Are you ready to rock?

Using the iPod in Your iPhone

To use your iPhone as an iPod, tap the Music icon in the bottom-right corner of the Home screen. At the bottom of the screen, you should see five icons: Radio, Playlists, Artists, Songs, and More. If you don't see these icons, tap the Back button in the top-left corner of the screen (the one that looks like a little arrow pointing to the left).

Or, if you're holding your iPhone sideways (the long edges parallel to the ground), rotate it 90 degrees so that it's upright (the short edges parallel to the ground).

iTunes Radio

If you're familiar with "streaming" Internet radio services like Pandora, you're already familiar with the premise behind the new iTunes Radio feature in iOS 7: Tap the Radio icon at the bottom of the screen, and you can listen to all sorts of music wherever you have a Wi-Fi or cellular data connection. iTunes Radio offers preconfigured radio "stations" (like The Beatles Radio, a personal favorite), or you can search for specific songs, artists, or genres of music. You can also create your own custom station, and iTunes Radio suggests additional songs based on the music you add!

To begin listening, tap a Featured station from the list. To create your own station, tap the New Station thumbnail in the list and choose a musical genre as your starting point (or throw caution utterly to the wind by tapping the Search box and typing in the name of a favorite song or artist).

Playlists

Tap the Playlists icon at the bottom of the screen and a list of playlists appears. If you don't have any playlists on your iPhone, don't sweat it. Just know that if you had some, this is where they'd be. (Playlists let you organize songs around a particular theme or mood: opera arias, romantic ballads, British Invasion, whatever.)

Tap a playlist, and you see a list of the songs it contains. If the list is longer than one screen, flick upward to scroll down. Tap a song in the list and it plays — after the song is over, your iPhone continues with the next song in the playlist. That's all there is to selecting and playing a song from a playlist.

Artistic license

Now let's find and play a song by the artist's name instead of by playlist. Tap the Artists icon at the bottom of the screen and an alphabetical list of artists appears.

If the list is longer than one screen, you can, of course, flick upward to scroll down or flick downward to scroll up. But there are easier ways to find an artist. . . .

At the top of the list, above the letter A, you see a search field. Tap it, and type the name of the artist you want to find, as shown in Figure 4-1. Now tap the Search button to see a list of all matching artists.

Another way to find an artist is to tap one of the little letters on the right side of the screen to jump directly to artists that start with that letter.

 Notice that a magnifying glass appears above the *A* on the right side of the screen. Tap it to jump directly to the search field.

Song selection

Next, let's find a song by its title and play it. Tap the Songs icon at the bottom of the screen and a list of songs appears. You find songs the same ways you find artists: Flick upward or downward to scroll; use the search field at the top of the list; or tap a little letter on the right side of the screen.

Figure 4-1: Type the name of an artist or album in the search field.

Taking Control of Your Tunes

Now that you have the basics down, take a look at some other things you can do when your iPhone is in its iPod mode.

Album selection

Your iPhone also groups your music by albums. Tap the More icon at the bottom of the screen and then tap Albums — a list of albums is displayed, complete with cover art. Again, use the now-familiar Music controls to navigate through the list: Flick upward or downward to scroll; use the search field at the top of the list; or tap a little letter on the right side of the screen.

When you've found the album that fits your mood, tap it to display the songs and then tap the desired track to play it.

Go with the (Cover) Flow

Finding tracks by playlist, artist, or song is cool, but finding them with Cover Flow is even cooler. Cover Flow lets you browse your music collection by its album artwork. To use Cover Flow, turn your iPhone sideways (long edges parallel to the ground). As long as you aren't browsing or viewing video (and, of course, you tapped the Music icon on the Home screen so that your iPhone behaves like an iPod), Cover Flow fills the screen, as shown in Figure 4-2.

Flipping through your cover art in Cover Flow is simple. All you have to do is drag or flick your finger left or right on the screen and the covers go flying by. Flick or drag quickly and the covers whiz by; flick or drag slowly and the covers move leisurely.

Figure 4-2: Go with the Cover Flow.

Try it — you'll like it! Here's how to put Cover Flow to work for you:

- ✔ **To see tracks (songs) on an album:** Tap any cover thumbnail. The track list appears.

- ✔ **To play a track:** Tap its name in the list. If the list is long, scroll by dragging or flicking up and down on it.

- ✔ **To go back to Cover Flow:** Tap anywhere outside the cover art display at the left of the screen.

- ✔ **To play or pause the current song:** Tap the Play/Pause button in the lower-left corner.

If no cover art exists for an album in your collection, the iPhone displays a plain-looking cover decorated with the album title.

And that, friends, is all there is to the iPhone's cool Cover Flow mode.

Flow's not here right now

As you can see earlier in this chapter, when you hold your iPhone vertically (the short edges are parallel to the ground) and tap the Playlists, Artists, Albums, or Songs button, you see a list rather than Cover Flow.

Along the same lines, when you're listening to music, the controls you see are different depending on which way you hold your iPhone. When you hold your iPhone vertically, as shown in Figure 4-3, you see controls that don't appear when you hold your iPhone sideways. Furthermore, the controls you see when viewing the Playlists, Artists, Albums, or Songs lists are slightly different from the controls you see when a song is playing.

 Here's another cool side effect of holding your iPhone vertically: If you add lyrics to a song in iTunes on your computer (by selecting the song, choosing File➪Get Info, and then pasting or typing the lyrics into the Lyrics tab in the Info window), the lyrics are displayed along with the cover art.

Here's how to use the controls that appear when the iPhone is vertical:

- ✔ **Back button:** Tap to return to whichever list you used last — Playlists, Artists, Albums, or Songs.

- ✔ **Switch to Track List button:** Tap to switch to a list of tracks.

 If you don't see the next three controls — the Repeat button, the Scrubber bar, and the Shuffle button — tap the Done button at the top-right corner of the screen to make them appear.

Switch to Track List

Scrubber bar

Next Track/Fast Forward

Volume

Shuffle

Repeat   Create   Play/Pause

Restart/Previous Track/Rewind

Figure 4-3: Hold your iPhone vertically when you play a track and you see these controls.

✔ **Repeat button:** Tap once to repeat songs in the current album or list. The button turns blue. Tap it again to play the current song repeatedly; the blue button displays the number 1 when it's in this mode. Tap the button again to turn off this feature. The button goes back to its original gray color.

✔ **Scrubber bar:** Drag the little dot (the playhead) along the Scrubber bar to skip to any point within the song.

✔ **Create:** Tap this button to generate a Genius playlist containing songs from your iPhone's music library that are similar to the song currently playing — typically, a Genius playlist has songs from the same genre. You can also use the song (or the song's artist) as the basis for a new iTunes Radio station.

✔ **Shuffle button:** Tap once to shuffle songs and play them in random order.

As you see later in this chapter, another setting, when enabled, lets you shake your iPhone from side-to-side to shuffle and play a different song at random.

✔ **Restart/Previous Track/Rewind button:** Tap once to go to the beginning of the track. Tap this button twice to go to the start of the preceding track in the list. Touch and hold this button to rewind the song at double speed.

✔ **Play/Pause button:** Tap to play or pause the song.

✔ **Next Track/Fast Forward button:** Tap to skip to the next track in the list. Touch and hold this button to fast-forward through the song at double speed.

✔ **Volume control:** Drag the little dot left or right to reduce or increase the volume level.

If you're using the headset included with your iPhone, you can squeeze the mic to pause, and squeeze it again to play. You can also squeeze it twice in rapid succession to skip to the next song. Sweet!

When you tap the Switch to Track List button, the iPhone screen and the controls change, as shown in Figure 4-4.

Figure 4-4: Tap the Switch to Track List button and these new controls appear.

Here's how to use *those* controls:

 ✔ **Done button:** Tap this button to return to the Now Playing screen for the current track.

 ✔ **Rating button:** Tap the Rating button, and a series of five dots appear below the track that's currently playing. Drag across the rating dots to rate the current track using zero to five stars.

The tracks are the songs in the current list (album, playlist, or artist, for example), and the current track indicator shows you which song is now playing (or paused). Tap any song in a track list to play it.

And that, gentle reader, is all you need to know to enjoy listening to music (and audiobooks) on your iPhone.

Customizing Your Audio Experience

In this section, you find a bunch of stuff you can do to make your listening experience more enjoyable.

Finding even more choices

If you prefer to browse your audio collection by criteria other than playlist, artist, album, or song, you can tap the More button in the lower-right corner of the screen (the More list appears) and tap a choice in the list — albums, compilations, composers, and genres. Your audio collection is organized by your criterion. Tap Shared to display any iTunes libraries being shared between your computers and iOS devices.

Wait — there's more. You can swap out the Playlists, Artists, Songs, and Video buttons for ones that better suit your needs. For example, if you often switch genres but seldom listen exclusively to a single artist, you can replace the Artists button with the Genres button.

Here's how:

1. **Tap the More button in the lower-right corner of the screen.**

2. **Tap the Edit button in the upper-right corner of the screen.**

3. **Drag any button on the screen — Playlists, Artists, Songs, Albums, Genres, Composers, Compilations — to the button at the bottom of the screen that you want to replace.**

4. **(Optional) Rearrange the five buttons now by dragging them to the left or right.**

5. **When you have everything just the way you like it, tap the Done button to return to the More list.**

 If you choose to replace one of the buttons this way, the item you replaced is available by tapping the More button and choosing the item that corresponds to the button you replaced in the More list.

Setting preferences

You can change a few preference settings to customize your iPhone-as-an-iPod experience.

Play all songs at the same volume level

The iTunes Sound Check option automatically adjusts the level of songs so that they play at the same volume relative to each other. That way, one song never blasts out your ears even if the recording level is much louder than that of the song before or after it. To tell the iPhone to use these volume settings, you first have to turn on the feature in iTunes on your computer. Here's how to do that:

1. **Choose iTunes➪Preferences (Mac) or Edit➪ Preferences (PC).**

2. **Click the Playback tab.**

3. **Select the Sound Check check box to enable it.**

Now you need to tell the iPhone to use the Sound Check settings from iTunes. Here's how to do *that:*

1. **Tap the Settings icon on the iPhone's Home screen.**
2. **Tap Music in the list of settings.**
3. **Tap Sound Check to turn it on.**

Choose an equalizer setting

An *equalizer* increases or decreases the relative levels of specific frequencies to enhance the sound you hear. Some equalizer settings emphasize the bass (low end) notes in a song; other equalizer settings make the higher frequencies more apparent. The iPhone has more than a dozen equalizer presets, with names such as Acoustic, Bass Booster, Bass Reducer, Dance, Electronic, Pop, and Rock. Each one is ostensibly tailored to a specific type of music.

The way to find out whether you prefer using equalization is to listen to music while trying out different settings. To do that, first start listening to a song you like. Then, while the song is playing, follow these steps:

1. **Tap the Home button on the front of your iPhone.**
2. **Tap the Settings icon on the Home screen.**
3. **Tap Music in the list of settings.**
4. **Tap EQ in the list of Music settings.**
5. **Tap different EQ presets (Pop, Rock, R&B, or Dance, for example) and listen carefully to the way it changes how the song sounds.**
6. **When you find an equalizer preset that you think sounds good, tap the Home button and you're finished.**

If you don't like any of the presets, tap Off at the top of the EQ list to turn off the equalizer.

Set a volume limit for music (and videos)

You can instruct your iPhone to limit the loudest listening level for audio. To do so, here's the drill:

1. **Tap the Settings icon on the Home screen.**

2. **Tap Music in the list of settings.**

3. **Tap Volume Limit in the list of Music settings.**

4. **Drag the slider to adjust the maximum volume level to your liking.**

The Volume Limit setting only limits the volume of music. It doesn't apply to podcasts or audiobooks. And, although the setting works with any headset, headphones, or speakers plugged into the headset jack on your iPhone, it doesn't affect sound played on your iPhone's internal speaker.

Enable the shake to shuffle option

Shake to Shuffle is an unusual setting that does just what its name implies — lets you shake your iPhone to listen to a different song selected at random. Here's how to enable this setting:

1. **Tap the Settings icon on the Home screen.**

2. **Tap Music in the list of settings.**

3. **Tap the Shake to Shuffle to turn it on.**

Shake to shuffle. How can you not love a feature like that?

Making a playlist

Of course you can make playlists in iTunes and sync them with your iPhone, but you can also create playlists on your iPhone when you're out and about. Here's how:

1. **Tap the Music icon in the lower-right corner of the Home screen.**
2. **Tap the Playlists button at the bottom of the screen.**
3. **Tap the New Playlist item.**

   Music displays a New Playlist box.

4. **Type a name for your new playlist and tap Save.**

   An alphabetical list of all songs on your iPhone appears. To the right of each song is a little plus sign.

5. **Tap the plus sign next to a song name to add the song to your new playlist.**
6. **Tap the Done button in the upper-right corner.**

If you create a new playlist and then sync your iPhone with your computer, that playlist is saved both on the iPhone and in iTunes on your computer.

The playlists remain until you delete them from iTunes on your computer. To do that, select the playlist's name in the source list and then press Delete or Backspace. You can also delete a playlist from the Playlist screen — swipe from right to left across the playlist name, and a Delete button appears. Tap it to delete that playlist.

You can also edit the playlist you've created. To do so, tap the Playlists button at the bottom of the screen, tap the name of the playlist you've created, and tap the Edit button. Then do one of the following:

✔ **To move a song up or down in the playlist:** A little icon with three gray bars appears to the right of each song. Drag the icon up to move the song higher in the list or drag down to move the song lower in the list.

✔ **To add more songs to the playlist:** Tap the plus button in the upper-left corner.

✔ **To delete a song from the playlist:** Tap the minus sign to the left of the song name and then tap the Delete button. Note that deleting a song from the playlist doesn't remove the song from your iPhone.

When you finish editing, tap the Done button.

That's all you have to do to create and manage your own custom playlists.

Use your voice to control your iPod

If you have an iPhone 3GS, 4, 4S, 5, or 5s/c, you can boss your music around using nothing but your voice. Hold down the Home button for a few seconds until the Voice Control screen (iPhone 3GS and 4) or Siri screen (iPhone 4S, 5, and 5s/c) appears. Here are the things you can say:

✔ **To play an album, artist, or playlist:** Say "Play." Then say "album," "artist," or "playlist" and the name.

✔ **To Shuffle the current playlist:** Say "Shuffle."

✔ **To find out more about the currently playing song:** Say "What's playing," "What song is this," "Who sings this song," or "Who is this song by."

And hey, because your iPod happens to be an iPhone, you won't look stupid talking to it!

Finding Stuff to Watch

The iPhone 5s isn't going to replace a wall-sized high-definition television as the centerpiece of your home theater. But with its glorious widescreen 4-inch display — watching movies and other videos on the iPhone can be a cinematic delight.

The video you'll watch on the iPhone generally falls into one of three categories:

✔ **Movies, TV shows, and music videos that you've downloaded directly to your iPhone or that reside in iTunes software on your PC or Mac that you synchronize with your iPhone.** You can watch these by tapping the Video icon on the Home screen.

The iTunes Store features dedicated sections for purchasing episodes of TV shows and movies. A typical price as of this writing is $2.99 per episode for TV shows and $9.99 to $14.99 for feature films.

You can also rent some movies, typically for $2.99 or $3.99. You have 30 days to begin watching a rented flick, and 24 hours to finish once you've started. Such films appear in their own Rented Movies section on the video list. The number of days before your rental expires is displayed.

✔ **The boatload of video podcasts, just about all of them free, featured in the iTunes Store.** Podcasts started out as another form of Internet radio; but instead of listening to live streams, you downloaded files onto your computer or iPod to take in at your leisure. You watch podcasts using the Podcasts app (available in iOS 6 and 7).

✔ **Movies you've created in iMovie software or other software on the Mac or other programs on the PC.** All other videos you have downloaded from the Internet are included.

 You may have to prepare these videos so that they'll play on your iPhone. To do so, highlight the video in question after it resides in your iTunes library. Go to the File menu in iTunes, choose Create New Version and click Create iPod or iPhone Version.

Playing Video

Now that you know what you want to watch, here's how to watch it:

1. **On the Home screen, tap the Videos icon.**

   Your list of videos pops up. Videos are segregated by category — Movies, TV Shows, Music Videos, and Shared, although other categories such as Rented Movies may also appear.

2. **Flick your finger to scroll through the list and then tap the video you want to play.**

   When you tap a listing, you'll see plot details and the length of the video.

3. **Tap the Play button.**

   You may see a spinning circle for just a moment and then the video will begin.

4. **Turn the device to its side because the iPhone plays video only in landscape, or widescreen, mode.**

   For movies, this is a great thing. You can watch flicks as the filmmaker intended, in a cinematic *aspect ratio*.

5. **Now that the video is playing, tap the screen to display the controls shown in Figure 4-5.**

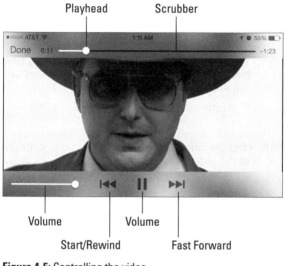

Figure 4-5: Controlling the video.

6. **Tap these controls as needed:**

- To play or pause the video, tap the Play/ Pause button.

- Drag the volume slider to the right to raise the volume and to the left to lower it. Alternatively, use the physical Volume buttons to control the audio levels. If the video is oriented properly, the buttons are to the bottom left of the iPhone.

- Tap the Restart/Rewind button to restart the video or tap and hold the same button to rewind.

• Tap and hold the Fast Forward button to advance the video. You can skip ahead also by dragging the playhead along the Scrubber bar.

7. **Tap the screen again to make the controls go away (or just wait for them to go away on their own).**

8. **Tap Done when you're finished watching (you have to summon the controls again if they're not already present).**

   You return to the iPhone's video menu screen.

To delete a video manually, tap the Edit button and then tap the small black Delete button that materializes at the corner of each thumbnail.

Chapter 5

You Oughta Be in Pictures

*T*he iPhone is a pretty spectacular photo viewer, even if you might not want to rely on its 5-megapixel (iPhone 4) or 8-megapixel (iPhone 4S/5/5s/5c) built-in digital camera for snapping pictures during an African safari, say, or even Junior's fast-paced soccer game. In steady hands, the iPhone can produce perfectly acceptable photos and your own blockbuster video. And with the iPhone, you can now shoot your own panoramic and square photos! Over the next few pages, you discover how best to exploit the iPhone's camera.

Taking Your Best Shot

Like many applications on the iPhone, you find the Camera application icon on the Home screen. Unless you've moved things around, it's positioned on the upper row of icons all the way to the right and adjacent to its next-of-kin, the Photos icon. We tap both icons throughout this chapter. Go ahead and snap an image now:

1. **Tap the Camera icon on the Home screen.**

2. **Keep your eyes fixed on the iPhone's display.**

   Your iPhone's screen acts as a window into what the camera lens sees. In case you were wondering, the primary camera lens is hiding behind the small foxhole at the top-left corner of the back of the iPhone.

   There's also a second camera lens on the front of the iPhone 4, 4S, 5, and 5s/c, facing you. If you'd like to use that camera instead (for an attractive self-portrait), tap the Switch Cameras icon at the top-right corner of the Camera app screen.

3. **Aim the camera, using the iPhone 5's 4-inch display as your viewfinder.**

4. **When you like what you see in the frame, tap the circular "shutter button" icon at the bottom of the screen (see Figure 5-1) to snap the picture.**

   You'll experience momentary shutter lag, so be sure to remain still. When the shutter reopens, you see the image you have just shot for just a second. Then the screen again functions as a viewfinder so that you can capture your next image. That's it; you've snapped your very first iPhone picture.

5. **Repeat Steps 3 and 4 to capture more images.**

—Switch
cameras
icon

Tap for preview of   Shutter button
last picture taken

Figure 5-1: Say "Cheese."

    If you position the iPhone sideways while snapping an image, the picture is saved in landscape mode.

    You also find the Camera icon on your Lock screen. There's no need to unlock your iPhone (or even tap the Camera icon on the Home screen) to take a quick snapshot. From the Lock screen, swipe upward on the Camera button.

The iPhone Camera app shutter button is super-sensitive. Be careful; a gentle tap is all that's required. If you have trouble keeping the camera steady, try this trick. Instead of tapping the Camera icon at the bottom of the screen, keep your finger pressed against the icon and only *release* it when you're ready to snap an image.

 With the iPhone 4, 4S, 5, and 5s/c you can take advantage of a feature dubbed *Tap to Focus*. Normally, the camera on these models focuses on a subject in the center of the display, which you're reminded of when you momentarily see a square in the middle of the screen. But if you tap elsewhere in the frame, perhaps on the face of your kid in the background, the iPhone shifts its focus there, adjusting the exposure and what photographers refer to as the *white balance*. For another moment or so, you see a new, smaller square over the child's face.

If you're running iOS 6 or 7, the iPhone 4S, 5, and 5s/c can take *panoramic* photos that encompass several screens — up to 240 degrees! To take a panoramic photo, swipe the Mode control that appears above the shutter button to the left to set the Camera mode to Pano. Follow the on-screen instructions and move your iPhone slowly and continuously from left to right across the breadth of your subject. The Camera app provides a visual aid to help you maintain a steady image — keep the arrow centered on the line that appears. To finish the shot, either move through the entire 240 degrees, or tap the Camera shutter button.

iOS 7 introduces the *square* Camera mode, which — as the name suggests — produces an image that's perfect for use in any app that prefers photos in a square format (think Facebook posts). Swipe the Mode control to the left or right as necessary to set the Camera mode to Square, and you see the viewfinder switch to the square format.

 With the debut of iOS 7, you can immediately apply filters to your photos, as you take them!

For example, suppose you find a subject that would look great as an old-fashioned black-and-white image; tap the Filters icon at the bottom-right corner of the Camera screen, and a grid of nine filter thumbnails displays. Tap the filter you want to use, and Camera adds that filter to your viewfinder. Now take your photo as you normally would, and enjoy the striking results. (If you decide you'd rather not use a filter after all, just tap None in the center of the grid.)

Importing Pictures

You don't have to use only the iPhone's digital camera to get pictures onto the device, of course. You can also synchronize photos from a PC or Macintosh using the Photos tab in the iTunes iPhone pane, which is described in Chapter 2.

Apple also offers a feature called *Photo Stream*, which works with iPhoto (version 9.2 or later) to wirelessly push any photos you take on your iPhone to all of your other iOS 5 (and later) devices (as well as your Mac or PC). Naturally, the reverse works like a charm as well: Your iPhone is automatically updated with the latest photos from your computer and other devices running iOS 5 or later. To turn on this magic, tap Settings and tap iCloud, tap Photos, then tap the My Photo Stream switch to enable the feature. (You can also enable Shared Photo Streams in iPhoto and from the Photos app, which you can use to distribute your photos to specific people and groups.)

When the iPhone is connected to your computer with the USB cable, click the Photos tab in the iTunes iPhone pane. Then click the appropriate check boxes to specify the pictures and photos you want to synchronize. Or choose All Photos, Albums, Events, and Faces if you have enough storage on the iPhone.

Syncing pictures and video is a two-way process, so photos and video captured with the iPhone's digital camera can also end up in the media library on your computer.

 Mac users: Connecting the iPhone with photos or videos in the Camera Roll usually launches iPhoto in addition to iTunes.

Where Did My Pictures Go?

So where exactly do your pictures hang out on the iPhone? The ones you snapped on iPhone end up in a photo album dubbed the *Camera Roll.* Of course, the photos you import are readily available (and grouped in the same albums they were on the computer). Here's how to get to your pix:

1. **From the Camera application, tap the Preview icon at the lower-left corner of the Camera screen (refer to Figure 5-1).**

   The viewfinder is replaced by the last image you shot, and you see the Camera Roll controls. If you don't see the Camera Roll controls, tap the screen.

2. **Tap the Camera Roll button at the upper-left corner of the screen, which shows the Camera Roll — thumbnail images of the photos and videos you've shot with the iPhone (see Figure 5-2).**

3. **Browse through the thumbnail images in the album until you find the picture you want to display.**

   If the thumbnail you have in mind doesn't appear on this screen, flick your finger up or down to scroll through the pictures rapidly or use a slower dragging motion to review the images more deliberately.

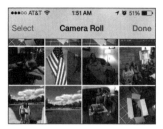

Figure 5-2: Your pictures at a glance.

4. **Tap the appropriate thumbnail.**

   The picture you've selected fills the screen and the Camera Roll controls re-appear (see Figure 5-3).

5. **To make the controls disappear, tap the screen again.**

6. **To transform the iPhone back into a picture-taker rather than a picture-viewer, make sure the picture controls are displayed and then tap the Done button at the upper right.**

   Note that this option is available only if you arrived at the Camera Roll from the Camera application. If you didn't, you have to back out of this application altogether and tap the Home button and then the Camera application icon to call the iPhone's digital camera back into duty.

7. **To return to the thumbnails view of your Camera Roll or the thumbnails for any of your other albums, make sure the picture controls are displayed. Then tap the Camera Roll button at the upper left.**

   The Camera Roll button will carry the name of one of your other photo albums if you're trying to return to that collection of pictures instead.

Figure 5-3: Picture controls.

Admiring Pictures

Photographs are meant to be seen, of course, not buried in the digital equivalent of a shoebox. And the iPhone affords you some neat ways to manipulate, view, and share your best photos.

You already know (from the preceding section) how to find a photo and view it full-screen and bring up picture controls. But you can do a lot of maneuvering of your pictures without summoning those controls. Here are some options:

✔ **Skipping ahead or viewing the previous picture:** Flick your finger left or right, or tap the left or right arrow control.

✔ **Landscape or portrait:** When you turn the iPhone sideways, the picture automatically reorients itself from portrait to landscape mode. Pictures shot in landscape mode fill the screen when you rotate the iPhone.

✔ **Zoom:** Double-tap to zoom in on an image and make it larger. Do so again to zoom out and make it smaller. Alternatively, take your thumb and index finger and pinch to zoom in, or unpinch to zoom out.

✔ **Pan and scroll:** After you zoom in on a picture, drag it around the screen with your finger to bring the part of the image you most care about front and center.

Launching Slideshows

If you store a lot of photographs on your computer, you may be familiar with running slideshows of those images. It's a breeze to replicate the slideshow experience on the iPhone:

1. **Choose your Camera Roll (from the Camera app) another album or collection (from the Photos app).**

   Tap the Photos icon from the Home screen or tap the Camera Roll button in the Camera application.

2. **Tap the thumbnail of the photo where the slideshow should begin.**

3. **Tap the Share button at the bottom-left corner of the thumbnails screen and then tap the Slideshow button.**

Your iPhone displays the Slideshow Options screen.

4. **Specify the slideshow settings.**

These include:

- **Transitions:** This effect is the one you see when you move from one photo to the next. You have five choices (cube, dissolve, ripple, wipe across, wipe down).

- **Play Music:** If you enable this option, you see the Music item appear. Tap the Music item and you can select a song from your iPhone's Music library.

5. **Tap Start Slideshow and you're finished.**

Enjoy the show.

Special slideshow effects

You can alter the length of time each slide is shown, change the transition effects between pictures, and display images in random order.

From the Home screen, tap Settings and then scroll down and tap Photos & Camera. Then tap any of the following to make changes:

- ✔ **Play Each Slide For:** You have five choices (2 seconds, 3 seconds, 5 seconds, 10 seconds, 20 seconds). When you're finished, tap the Photos button to return to the main Settings screen for Photos.

- ✔ **Repeat:** If this option is turned on, the slideshow continues to loop until you stop it. If it's turned off, the slideshow for your Camera Roll or album plays just once. The Repeat control may be counterintuitive. If Off is showing, tap it to turn on the Repeat function. If On is showing, tap it to turn off the Repeat function.

✔ **Shuffle:** Turning on this feature plays photos in random order. As with the Repeat feature, tap Off to turn on shuffle or tap On to turn off random playback.

Tap the Home button to leave the settings and return to the Home screen.

Deleting Pictures

Some pictures are meant to be seen. Others, well . . . you can't get rid of them fast enough. Fortunately, the iPhone makes it a cinch to bury the evidence:

1. **From the Camera Roll, tap the objectionable photograph.**

2. **Tap to display the picture controls, provided they're not already displayed.**

3. **Tap the trash can icon.**

4. **Tap Delete Photo (or Cancel if you change your mind).**

   The photo gets sucked into the trash can and mercifully disappears.

More (Not So) Stupid Picture Tricks

You can take advantage of the photos on the iPhone in a few more ways. In each case, you tap the desired picture and make sure the picture controls are displayed. Then tap the icon that looks like an arrow trying to escape from a rectangle. That displays the choices shown in Figure 5-4 (note that you may have to swipe the two rows of buttons to the left to see all the choices I list here).

Figure 5-4: Look at what else I can do!

Here's what each choice does:

- **AirDrop:** Transfer the displayed picture to another AirDrop-compatible device that's running iOS 7 or later. Tap the device that should receive the photo — the recipient is prompted for approval, of course. (Don't forget, both Wi-Fi and Bluetooth must be enabled for AirDrop to work.)

- **Use as Wallpaper:** When you tap the Use as Wallpaper button, you see what the present image looks like as the iPhone's background picture. And you're given the opportunity to move the picture around and resize it. When you're satisfied with what the wallpaper will look like, tap the Set button — you can choose to use the new image as your Lock screen or Home screen wallpaper, or throw all caution to the wind and use it for both. Per usual, you also have the option to tap Cancel.

✔ **Mail:** Some photos are so precious that you just have to share them with family members and friends. When you tap Mail, the picture is automatically embedded in the body of an outgoing e-mail message. Use the virtual keyboard to enter the e-mail addresses, subject line, and any comments you want to add. (Check out Chapter 6 for more info on using e-mail.)

You can also press and hold the screen until a Copy button appears. Tap that button, and now you can paste the image into an e-mail.

✔ **iCloud:** Tap this button and you can distribute the photo to a new or existing Shared Photo Stream.

✔ **Message:** Apple and your provider support picture messaging by way of *MMS* (Multimedia Messaging Service) — or, if you're sending this photo to another device running iOS 5 or later, you can use a free iMessage instead. Tap the Message option, and the picture is embedded in your outgoing message; you merely need to enter the phone number (or e-mail address) of the device to which you're sending the picture.

✔ **Assign to Contact:** If you assign a picture to someone in your Contacts list, this image pops up whenever you receive a call from that person. To make it happen, tap Assign to Contact. Your list of contacts appears on the screen. Scroll up or down the list to find the person who matches the picture of the moment. As with the wallpaper example, you can drag and resize the picture to get it just right. Then tap Set Photo.

You can also assign a photo to a contact by starting out in Contacts. As a refresher, start by tapping Phone and then tapping Contacts. From Contacts, choose the person, tap Edit, and then tap Add Photo. At that point, you can take a new picture with the iPhone's digital camera or select an existing portrait from one of your onboard picture albums.

To change the picture you assigned to a person, tap her name in the Contacts list, tap Edit, and then tap the person's thumbnail picture, which also carries the label Edit. From there, you can take another photo with the iPhone's digital camera, select another photo from one of your albums, edit the photo you're already using (by resizing and dragging it to a new position), or delete the photo you no longer want.

✔ **AirPlay:** Tap this button to display the photo on your Apple TV (or any device that supports AirPlay display mirroring).

✔ **Print:** Tap this button to send the photo to a printer that supports AirPrint. Your iPhone gives you the option of printing multiple copies, too.

✔ **Facebook:** If you've configured a Facebook account within Settings and you've installed the Facebook app on your iPhone, tap this button to create a new shared photo on your timeline.

✔ **Flickr:** After you've added a Flickr account within Settings, tap this button to share the photo on Flickr.

 ✔ **Twitter:** If you have at least one Twitter account
   configured in the Twitter pane within Settings
   (and you've installed the Twitter app), you can
   add the photo to a tweet.

 Before leaving this photography section, we
   want to steer you to the App Store, which we
   explore in Chapter 7. As of this writing, hun-
   dreds of photography-related applications,
   many free, are available.

We also want to point out that many picture apps
take advantage of the iPhone's location smarts. You
can *geotag* pictures with the location in which you
shot them. The first few times you use the iPhone's
Camera application, it asks for your permission to use
your current location. Similarly, third-party apps ask
whether it's okay to use your location. iPhoto allows
you to display (and even browse) your photo library
for geotags. Later on, you might plot a picture's location on a map or use geotagged images to see where
friends or like-minded individuals are hanging out.

Shooting Video

The 3GS, 4, 4S, 5, and 5s/c all allow you to shoot
video — heck, the iPhone 4S, 5, and 5s/c even provide
full 1080p HD recording! Here's how to do it:

1. **Tap the Camera icon on the Home screen.**

2. **Swipe the Mode control all the way to the right
   to set the Camera mode to Video, as shown in
   Figure 5-5.**

   The shutter button turns into a red Record
   button.

Tap here for the   Tap here to start or stop
Camera Roll   capturing video

Figure 5-5: Lights, camera, action.

3. **Tap the Record button to begin shooting a scene. You can capture video in portrait or landscape mode.**

   The button turns into a square to indicate you're recording, and you see a counter timing the length of your video.

4. **When you're done, tap the red button again to stop the recording.**

   Your video is automatically saved to the Camera Roll, alongside any other saved videos and still pictures.

 The 3GS and later iPhones shoot video at up to 30 frames-per-second. That's tech jargon for *full-motion video,* and what it really means is your video won't be herky-jerky or look like it was shot in Jell-O.

Editing what you shot

Likely, you captured some really great photos and some stuff that belongs on the cutting room floor. That's not a problem because you can perform simple edits right on your iPhone 3GS or iPhone 4/4S/5/5s:

1. **Tap a video recording to bring up the on-screen controls shown in Figure 5-6.**

2. **Drag the start and end points along the timeline to select only the video you want to keep. Hold your finger over the section to expand the timeline to make it easier to apply your edits.**

   You can tap the Play button to preview the edit.

3. **Tap Trim to save your changes.**

   You have the option to trim the original clip, or to save the trimmed result as a new clip.

 If you choose Trim Original, make sure you're satisfied with your edit. You can't undo this action.

Figure 5-6: Trimming video.

Sharing video

Unlike other video on your iPhone, you can play back what you've just shot in portrait or landscape mode. And if the video is any good (and why wouldn't it be), you're likely going to want to share it with others. To do so, bring up the playback controls by tapping the screen; then tap the Share icon and choose how you'll share your latest Hollywood epic.

Chapter 6

Surfing the Net and Using E-Mail

. . . .

In This Chapter

▶ Surfing the Net

▶ Opening and displaying web pages

▶ Using Reminders to jog your memory

▶ Setting up your e-mail accounts

▶ Sending e-mail messages

▶ Reading and managing e-mail messages

. . . .

*F*or years, the cell-phone industry has been offering a watered-down mobile version of the
Internet, but the approaches have fallen far short of
what you've come to experience on your computer.
With the iPhone, however, Apple has managed to replicate the real-deal Internet. Web pages look like web
pages on a Windows PC or Macintosh, right down to
swanky graphics and pictures. In this chapter, you
find out how to navigate through cyberspace on
your iPhone.

Surfin' Safari

A version of Apple Safari web browser is a major reason the Net is the Net on the iPhone. Safari for the Mac and, more recently, for Windows, is one of the best web browsers in the computer business. In our view, it has no rival as a cell-phone browser.

Exploring the browser

It is worth starting your cyber-expedition with a quick tour of the Safari browser. Take a gander at Figure 6-1.

Blasting into cyberspace

When you tap the address field at the top of the Safari browser, the virtual keyboard appears. You may notice one thing about the keyboard right off the bat: the . (period) is on the virtual keyboard because you frequently use periods when you enter web addresses.

The moment you tap a single letter, you see a list of web addresses that match those letters. For example, if you tap the letter *E*, you may see web listings for EarthLink, eBay, and so on.

When you tap a letter, the iPhone makes suggestions either from the websites you've already bookmarked (and synced) from Safari or Internet Explorer on your computer or from your History list — those cyber-destinations you've recently hung your hat in.

Go ahead and open your first web page now:

1. **Tap the Safari icon at the bottom of the Home screen.**

2. **Tap the address field.**

If you can't see the address field, tap the site name at the top of the screen or flick down to scroll to the top of the screen.

3. **Begin typing the web address (URL) on the virtual keyboard that slides up from the bottom of the screen.**

Figure 6-1: The iPhone's Safari browser.

4. **Do one of the following:**

a. To accept one of the bookmarked (or other) sites that shows up on the list, merely tap the name.

Safari automatically fills in the URL in the address field and takes you where you want to go.

b. Keep tapping the proper keyboard characters until you've entered the complete web address for the site you have in mind, and then tap Go at the bottom-right corner of the keyboard.

It's not necessary to type www at the beginning of a URL. So if you want to visit `www.theonion.com` (for example), typing theonion.com is sufficient.

Even though Safari on the iPhone can render web pages the way they're meant to be displayed on a computer, you may run into a site that serves up the light, or mobile, version of the website. Graphics may be stripped down on such sites. (For example, CNN.com detects the mobile version of Safari when you visit and presents a simplified site.)

Seeing Pages More Clearly

Now that you know how to open up a web page, we'll show you how radically simple it is to zoom in on the pages to read what you want to read and see what you want to see, without enlisting a magnifying glass.

Try these neat tricks:

✔ **Double-tap the screen so that that portion of the text fills up the entire screen.** It takes just a second before the screen comes into focus. Check out Figure 6-2. It shows two views of the same *New York Times* web page. In the first view, you see what the page looks like when you first arrive. In the second, you see how the middle column takes over the screen after you double-tapped it. To return to the first view, double-tap the screen again.

✔ **Pinch the page.** Sliding your thumb and index finger together and then spreading them apart also zooms in and out of a page. Again, wait just a moment for the screen to come into focus.

✔ **Press down on a page and drag it in all directions, or flick through a page from top to bottom.**

Figure 6-2: A double-tap zooms in and out.

✔ **Rotate the iPhone to its side.** Watch what happens to the *National Geographic* website shown in Figure 6-3. It reorients from portrait to a wide-screen view. The keyboard is also wider, making it a little easier to enter a new URL.

Figure 6-3: Going wide.

Using the Reading List

The Safari Reading List enables you to save interesting pages you encounter during a surfing session for later reading. Tap the Action icon at the bottom of the Safari screen (it's the square with the arrow in the middle of the row) and tap Add to Reading List. You can do this as often as you like while surfing.

 You can also send a tweet or post on your Facebook page with a link to this site by tapping the Twitter or Facebook button.

To display the Reading List, tap the Bookmarks icon at the bottom of the screen (it looks like an open book) and choose Reading List. Tap a story to view the page, and the story is automatically removed from the list.

Putting Reminders to Work

It's time to banish that old appointment book (or even worse, that stack of tiny scraps of paper in your wallet or purse). With Reminders, your iPhone can hold your to-do list (and keep it updated automatically across all of your iOS devices using iCloud). Reminders works with OS X Calendar and Outlook too, keeping track of events between your computer and your iPhone.

To get started, tap the Reminders icon on the Home screen. You see the layout shown in Figure 6-4, which displays the lists you've created. To view your reminders, tap the desired list to expand it (Figure 6-4 shows two lists named Reminders and Work). To add a new reminder, tap the empty space at the bottom of the list and the virtual keyboard appears, enabling you to type the text of your reminder. When you're finished, tap the Done button at the upper-right corner. Now you can tap the item itself and then tap the Info icon, which displays the Details dialog; from here, you can set the date to display the reminder, and choose to be reminded when you enter or leave a location. If you choose a date for the reminder, you can specify whether this is a repeating event and create an audible alarm with a corresponding notification.

You can create a new list by tapping the New List tab at the top-level screen.

After you've taken care of a to-do item, you can tap the check box next to it to indicate that it's been completed. To delete a reminder, tap the Edit button on the top-level List screen. Tap the red circle with a minus sign and tap Delete.

To search for a specific reminder, tap the Search box field at the top of the screen and type the text you want to match.

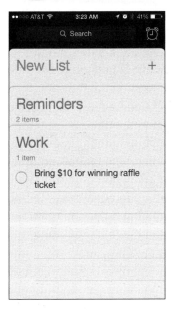

Figure 6-4: The Reminders screen.

Setting Up E-Mail

One of the niftiest things your iPhone can do is send and receive real, honest-to-gosh e-mail using Mail, its modern e-mail application. It's designed not only to send and receive text e-mail messages, but also to handle rich HTML e-mail messages — formatted e-mail messages complete with font and type styles and embedded graphics.

Furthermore, your iPhone can read several types of file attachments, including PDF, Microsoft Word, PowerPoint, and Excel documents, as well as stuff produced through Apple's own iWork software. Better still, all this sending and receiving of text, graphics, and documents can happen in the background, so you can surf the web or talk to a friend while your iPhone quietly and efficiently handles your e-mail behind the scenes.

To use Mail, you need an e-mail address. If you have broadband Internet access (that is, a cable modem or DSL), you probably received one or more e-mail addresses when you signed up. If you are one of the handful of readers who doesn't already have an e-mail account, you can get one for free from Yahoo! (http://mail.yahoo.com), Google (http://mail.google.com), Microsoft (http://outlook.com), AOL (www.aol.com), and many other service providers. (Apple also gives you a free iCloud e-mail address when you create an Apple ID.)

Set up your account the easy way

Chapter 2 explains the option of automatically syncing the e-mail accounts on your computer with your iPhone. If you chose that option, your e-mail accounts should be configured on your iPhone already. You may proceed directly to the "Sending E-Mail" section.

If you have not yet chosen that option but would like to set up your account the easy way now, go to Chapter 2 and read that section, sync your iPhone, and then you, too, may proceed directly to the "Sending E-Mail" section.

Set up your account the less easy way

If you don't want to sync the e-mail accounts on your computer, you can set up an e-mail account on your iPhone manually. It's not quite as easy as clicking a box and syncing your iPhone, but it's not rocket science either.

If you have no e-mail accounts on your iPhone, the first time you launch Mail you're walked through the following procedure. If you have one or more e-mail accounts on your iPhone already and want to add a new account manually, start by tapping Settings on the Home screen and then tap Mail, Contacts, Calendars, and Add Account.

You should now be staring at the Add Account screen. Proceed to one of the next two sections, depending on your e-mail account.

Yahoo!, Google, Microsoft, AOL, or iCloud.

If your account is with Yahoo!, Google (Gmail), AOL, Microsoft Exchange, Microsoft Outlook.com, or Apple's own iCloud service, tap the appropriate button on the Add Account screen. If your account is with a provider other than one of these six, tap the Other button and skip ahead to the next section.

Enter your name, e-mail address, and password, as shown in Figure 6-5 (these are the fields required for a Google Gmail account). There's a field for a description of this account (such as work or personal), but it tends to fill in automatically with the same contents in the Address field unless you tell it differently.

Tap the Next button in the top-right corner of the screen. You're finished. Your e-mail provider verifies your credentials. If you pass muster, that's all there is to setting up your account.

Another provider

If your e-mail account is with a provider other than Yahoo!, Google, AOL, Microsoft, or iCloud, you have a bit more work ahead of you. You're going to need a bunch of information about your e-mail account that you may not know or have handy.

We suggest that you skim the following instructions, note the items you don't know, and go find the answers before you continue. To find the answers, look at the documentation you received when you signed up for your e-mail account or visit the account provider's website and search there.

Here's how you set up an account:

1. **On the Add Account screen, tap the Other button.**

2. **Under Mail, tap Add Mail Account; fill in the appropriate Name, Address, Password, and Description fields, the same as if you were setting up an account with one of the providers mentioned earlier.**

3. **Tap Next.**

    With any luck, that's all you'll have to do, although you may have to endure a spinning cursor for a while as the iPhone attempts to retrieve information and validate your account with your provider. Otherwise, continue on with Step 4.

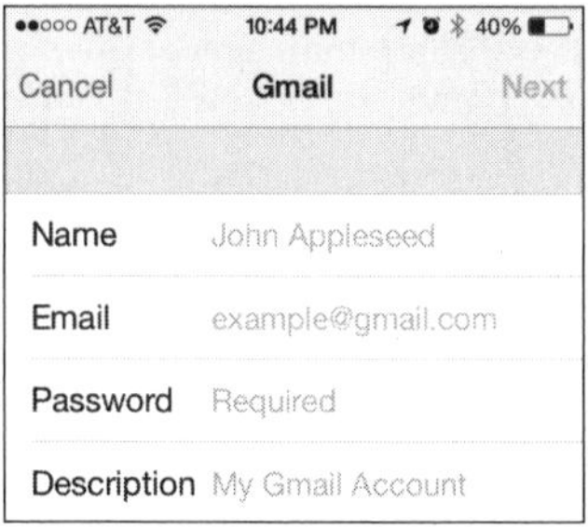

Figure 6-5: Just fill 'em in, tap Next, and you're ready to rock.

4. **Tap the button at the top of the screen that denotes the type of e-mail server this account uses: IMAP or POP.**

5. **Fill in the Internet host name for your incoming mail server, which should look something like mail.*providername*.com.**

6. **Fill in your username and password.**

7. **Enter the Internet host name for your outgoing mail server, which should look something like smtp.*providername*.com.**

   You may have to scroll down to the bottom of the screen to see the outgoing mail server fields.

8. **Enter your username and password in the provided fields.**

9. **Tap the Next button in the upper-right corner to create the account.**

 Some outgoing mail servers don't need your username and password. The fields for these items on your iPhone note that they are optional. Still, we suggest that you fill them in anyway. It will save you from having to add them later if your outgoing mail server *does* require an account name and password, which many do these days.

Sending E-Mail

Now that your account or accounts are set up, let's look at how to use your iPhone to send e-mail.

There are several subspecies of messages: pure text, text with a photo, a partially finished message you want to save and complete later (called a *draft*), a reply to an incoming message, forwarding an incoming message to someone else, and so on. The following sections examine these subsets one at a time.

Sending an all-text message

To compose a new e-mail message, tap Mail on your
Home screen. You should see a screen that looks
pretty much like the one in Figure 6-6 — if not, tap your
primary mail account name in the Accounts section.

Don't worry if yours doesn't look exactly like this or if
your folders have different names.

Now, to create a new message, follow these steps:

1. **Tap the New Message button (labeled in
   Figure 6-6) in the lower-right corner of the
   screen.**

2. **Type the names or e-mail addresses of the recipients in the To: field, or tap the + button to the
   right of To: to choose a contact or contacts from
   your iPhone's address book.**

3. **(Optional) Tap the field labeled Cc/Bcc/From:.
   Doing so breaks these out into separate Cc:,
   Bcc:, and From: fields.**

   The Cc/Bcc: label stands for *carbon copy/blind
   carbon copy.* If you haven't used Bcc: before, it
   enables you to include a recipient on the message that other recipients can't see has been
   included. Tap the respective Cc: or Bcc: field to
   type in names. Or tap the + that appears in those
   fields to add a contact.

    If you start typing an e-mail address, e-mail
   addresses that match what you've typed appear
   in a list below the To: or Cc: field. If the correct
   one is in the list, tap it to use it.

4. **Type a subject in the Subject field.**

   The subject is optional, but it's considered poor
   form to send an e-mail message without one.

5. **Type your message in the message area.**

The message area is immediately below the Subject field.

6. **Tap the Send button in the top-right corner of the screen.**

Your message will wing its way to its recipients almost immediately. If you are not in range of a Wi-Fi network, the AT&T EDGE network, or a 3G/4G/LTE data network when you tap Send, the message is sent the next time you are in range of one of these networks.

 Apple includes *landscape* keyboards within various applications, including Mail. So when you rotate the phone to its side, you can compose a new message using a wider-format virtual keyboard.

●●●○○ AT&T 🛜 ☀	3:25 AM	◢ ◉ ✳ 40% ▭
	Mailboxes	Edit

☐ All Inboxes		2 ›
☐ Gmail		›
☐ Books		2 ›
☐ iCloud		›
★ VIP		›

ACCOUNTS

8 Gmail		›
@ Books		2 ›
☁ iCloud		›

| Updated Just Now | 🖉 | —— New message |

Figure 6-6: The mailboxes screen.

Replying to or forwarding a message

When you receive a message and want to reply to it, open the message and then tap the Reply/Reply All/ Forward button, which looks like a curved arrow at the bottom of the screen, as shown in Figure 6-7. Then tap the Reply, Reply All, or Forward button — you can also print the message by tapping this button.

The Reply button creates a blank e-mail message addressed to the sender of the original message. The Reply All button creates a blank e-mail message addressed to the sender and all other recipients of the original message (the button only appears with multiple recipients). In both cases the subject is retained with a *Re:* prefix added. So if the original subject were *iPhone Tips,* the reply's subject is *Re: iPhone Tips.*

Tapping the Forward button creates an unaddressed e-mail message that contains the text of the original message. Add the e-mail address(es) of the person or people you want to forward the message to, and then tap Send. In this case, instead of a *Re:* prefix, the subject is preceded by *Fwd:*. So this time the subject would be *Fwd: iPhone Tips.*

 Don't forget that snappy Dictation key on your iPhone's virtual keyboard! If you're running iOS 5 (or later), tap the key with the microphone symbol and begin speaking. When you're through dictating the message, tap the Done button.

To send your reply or forwarded message, tap the Send button as usual.

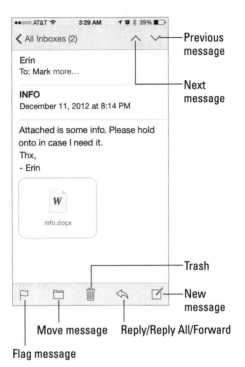

Figure 6-7: Reading and managing an e-mail message.

Working with Messages

The other half of the mail equation is receiving and reading the stuff. You can tell when you have unread mail by looking at the Mail icon, in the bottom of your Home screen. The cumulative number of unread messages appears in a little red circle on the top-right of the icon.

New message notifications also appear on the Notification Center — swipe down from the top of the screen to display it.

Reading messages

Tap the Mail icon now to summon the Mailboxes screen. At the top of the Inboxes section is the All Inboxes inbox, which, as its name suggests, is a repository for all the messages across all your accounts. To read your mail, tap an inbox: either All Inboxes to examine all your messages in one unified view or an individual account to check out messages from just that account.

Now tap a message to read it. When a message is on the screen, buttons for managing incoming messages appear below it.

Managing messages

When a message is on your screen, you can do the following in addition to reading it (all buttons are labeled in Figure 6-7):

- ✔ View the next message by tapping the next message button.

- ✔ View the previous message by tapping the previous message button (the downward-pointing arrow).

- ✔ Flag this message by tapping the Flag button, which looks like. . . well. . . a flag. You can choose to flag the message, mark it as unread, or move it to your Junk box for the current account. (When you flag a message, it appears in the Inbox list with a flag icon to the left of the entry. You can use flags to mark important messages that need immediate follow-up.)

✔ Move this message to another folder by tapping the Move Message button. When the list of folders appears, tap the folder where you want to file the message.

✔ Reply, reply to all, or forward this message (as discussed previously) by tapping the Reply/ Reply All/Forward button.

✔ Create a new e-mail message by tapping the New Message button.

You can delete e-mail messages without opening them in two ways:

✔ Swipe from right to left across the message entry and then tap the red Trash button that appears to the right of the message.

✔ Tap the Edit button in the upper-right corner of the screen and tap the little circle to the left of each message you want to remove. Tapping that circle puts a check mark in it. Tap the Trash button to erase all the messages you checked off. (Note that you can also mark multiple messages and move them to another folder using the same trick — just select the desired messages and tap Move instead!)

Chapter 7

Getting to Know iPhone Apps

A t this writing, more than 850,000 iPhone applications (*apps*) are available for downloading. Some are *third-party* (which means they don't come from Apple); some are free, others cost money; some are useful, others are lame; some are perfectly well-behaved, others quit unexpectedly (or worse).

You can obtain and install these applications directly to your iPhone or computer. In this chapter, we show you how to download them to your iPhone.

To use the App Store on your iPhone, it must be connected to the Internet. Before you can use the App Store on your iPhone, however, you first need an Apple ID. If you don't already have one, we suggest you launch iTunes on your computer and click the iTunes Store entry in the source list. Click Sign In near the upper-left corner of the iTunes Store window. Then click Create Apple ID and follow the on-screen instructions. Or, create your new account directly on your iPhone by following these steps:

1. **Tap the Settings icon on the Home screen.**

2. **Tap iTunes & App Stores in the list of settings.**

3. **Tap Create New Apple ID.**

4. **Follow the onscreen instructions.**

After the App Store knows who you are (and more importantly, knows your credit card number), tap the App Store icon on your Home screen and shop until you drop.

Finding Apps with Your iPhone

Using your iPhone to find apps is pretty darn easy. The only requirement is that you have an Internet connection of some sort — Wi-Fi or wireless data network — to browse, search, download, and install apps.

To get started, tap the App Store icon on your iPhone's Home screen. When you launch the App Store, you see five icons at the bottom of the screen, representing five ways to interact with the store, as shown in Figure 7-1.

The first two icons at the bottom of the screen — Featured and Top Charts — and the Categories button at the top left of the App Store screen offer three ways to browse the virtual shelves of the App Store.

Browsing the iPhone App Store

The Featured section includes several rows of apps — each row is a group of apps with a common theme, like New and Noteworthy or Great Games. Tap any of these app icons to display the details on that app.

Flick to the left across a row to display more icons in that group, or throw caution utterly to the wind and tap the See All link above that row (which displays the apps in that group in a full-screen display).

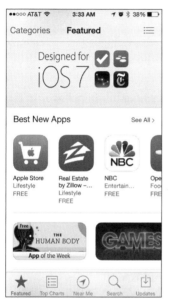

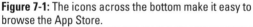

Figure 7-1: The icons across the bottom make it easy to browse the App Store.

The Categories screen works a little differently: Its main page contains no apps. Instead, it offers a list of categories such as Games, Entertainment, Utilities, Music, and Social Networking to name a few. Tap a category to see a page with rows displaying apps of that type. Each category's page has several rows, like Best New Apps, Essentials, Paid, and Free — to make your browsing easier.

The Top Charts section works much the same as the Featured section. Its three panels — Paid, Free, and Top Grossing — represent pages of the most popular apps that either cost money (paid and top grossing) or don't (free).

Each row displays a huge number of apps, but you see only three or four at a time on the screen. So remember to flick to the left if you want to see the others.

If you know exactly what you're looking for, instead of simply browsing you can tap the Search icon at the bottom of the App Store screen and type a word or phrase. The following sections show you how to find out more about a particular application.

Checking out the detail screen

To learn more about any application on any page, tap it, and a detail screen like the one shown in Figure 7-2 appears.

Remember that the application description on this screen was written by the developer and may be somewhat biased.

Reading reviews from your iPhone

At the top of the detail screen, you find a star rating for that application. Tap the Reviews tab to see a page full of them. At the bottom of that page is another link called More Reviews. Tap it to see (what else?) more reviews.

Figure 7-2: This is the detail screen for Remote, a free application from Apple that lets you control iTunes or Apple TV from your iPhone.

Downloading an App

To download an application to your iPhone, tap the price button near the top-right corner of its detail screen. In Figure 7-2, it's the rectangle that says *Free*. You may or may not be asked to type your Apple ID password before the App Store disappears and the next iPhone screen with an available spot — where the new application's icon will reside — takes its place. The new icon is slightly dimmed, with the word *Loading* or *Installing* beneath it and a nifty circular progress indicator to let you know how the download is progressing.

By the way, if the app happens to be rated 17+, you see a warning screen after you type your password. You have to click the OK button to confirm that you're over 17 before the app downloads.

The application is now on your iPhone, but it won't be copied to your iTunes library on your Mac or PC until your next sync (either using the cable or wirelessly). If your iPhone suddenly loses its memory (unlikely), or if you delete the application from your iPhone before you sync, that application is gone forever. That's the bad news.

The good news is that after you've paid for an app you can download it again if you need to — from iTunes on your computer or the Updates section of the App Store on your iPhone — and you won't have to pay for it again.

Chapter 8

Ten iPhone Tips

After spending quality time with our iPhones, we've discovered lots of helpful hints, tips, and shortcuts. In this chapter, we share some of our faves.

Do the Slide

This tip can help you type faster in two ways. First, it helps you type more accurately; second, it lets you type punctuation and numerals faster than ever before. We call this movement the *slide*.

To do the slide, you start by performing the first half of a tap. That is, you touch your finger to the screen but don't lift it up. Without lifting your finger, slide it onto the key you want to type. You'll know you're on the right key because it pops up — enlarges.

Try the slide during normal typing. Stab at a key; if you miss, rather than lifting your finger, backspacing, and trying again, do the slide onto the proper key. After you get the hang of it, you'll see that it saves time and improves your accuracy.

You can use the slide to save time with punctuation and numerals, too. The next time you need to type a punctuation mark or number, try this technique:

1. **Start a slide action with your finger on the 123 key (the key to the left of the Space key when the alphabetical keyboard is active).**

   This is a slide, not a tap, so don't lift your finger just yet.

2. **When the punctuation and numeric keyboard appears on-screen, slide your finger onto the punctuation mark or number you want to type.**

3. **Lift your finger.**

The cool thing is that the punctuation and numeric keyboard disappears and the alphabetical keyboard reappears — all without tapping the 123 key to display the punctuation and numeric keyboard and without tapping the ABC key (the key to the left of the Space key when the punctuation and numeric keyboard is active).

Use Auto Apostrophes

The auto-correction software on the iPhone is your friend. You can type *dont* to get to *don't*, and *cant* to get to *can't*. We know of at least one exception. The iPhone cannot distinguish between *it's,* the contraction of "it is," and *its,* the possessive adjective and possessive pronoun.

Make Rejection Work for You

If the auto-correct suggestion isn't the word you want, instead of ignoring it, reject it. Finish typing the word and then tap the *x* to reject the suggestion before you type another word. Doing so makes your iPhone more likely to accept your word the next time you type it.

View the iPhone's Capacity

When your iPhone is selected in the source list in iTunes, you see a colorful chart at the bottom of the screen that tells you how your iPhone's capacity is being used by your media and other data. Hover your cursor over any of the sections in the chart to see exactly how many items are included in that section, and how much of your valuable digital real estate those particular items are taking up. This can help you if you're trying to decide whether you need to convert your music to a lower bitrate, or if you need to convert your videos to standard definition.

URL and Phone Number Tricks

The iPhone does something special when it encounters a phone number or URL in e-mail and messages. The iPhone interprets as a phone number any sequence of numbers that looks like a phone number: 1-123-555-4567, 555-4567, 1.123.555.4567, and so on. The same goes for sequences of characters that look like a web address, such as www.websitename.com. When the iPhone sees what it assumes to be a URL, it appears as a blue link on your screen.

If you tap a phone number or URL sequence like the ones just shown, the iPhone does the right thing. It launches the Phone application and dials the number or launches Safari and takes you to the appropriate web page for a URL. That's useful, but somewhat expected. What's more useful and not so expected is the way Safari handles phone numbers and URLs.

When you encounter a phone number on a web page, give it a tap. A little dialog box appears on the screen displaying that phone number and offering you a choice of two buttons: Call or Cancel. Tap Call to switch to the Phone application and dial the number; tap Cancel to return to the web page.

Here's a cool Safari trick with links. If you press and hold on a link rather than tapping it, Safari shows you the underlying URL, and even offers to copy the URL, open it in a new page, or add it to your Reading list.

 You also see the underlying URL if you press and hold on a URL in Mail or Messages, which enables you to spot bogus links (often called *phishing* scams) without switching to Safari or actually visiting the URL.

Finally, here's one last trick. If you press and hold on most graphic images, a Save Image button appears. Tap it and the picture is saved to the Camera Roll in the Photos application. You can also copy the image for later pasting within another application!

Share the Love

Ever stumble on a web page you just have to share with a buddy? The iPhone makes it dead simple, using a veritable host of options! From the site in question, tap the action button at the bottom of the browser (which looks like a square sprouting an arrow).

To include the page in a Mail message, tap the Mail button. A mail message appears with the subject line pre-populated with the name of the website you're visiting, and the body of the message pre-populated with the URL. Just type something in the message body (or don't), supply your pal's e-mail address, and tap the Send button.

To share the page via AirDrop, tap the AirDrop icon for the target device. (Naturally, both devices should have AirDrop toggled on in the Control Center.)

The Action button also sports buttons for Twitter and Facebook — tap either button and you can immediately begin typing the body of your Twitter tweet or Facebook post. Again, the URL is included automatically.

Finally, tap Message to create a new text message with the URL, ready for you to address.

Choose a Safari Home Page

You may have noticed that there's no home page web site on the iPhone version of Safari as there is in the Mac and PC versions of the browser. Instead, when you tap the Safari icon, you return to the last site you visited.

You can create an icon for the page you want to use as your home page by creating a *web clip* of a web page. Here's how to do it:

1. **Open the web page you want to use as your home page and tap the action button.**
2. **Tap the Add to Home Screen button.**
3. **Type a short name for the icon and tap Add at the top-right corner of the screen.**

An icon to open this page appears on the first screen with an empty spot on your iPhone.

4. **Tap this new web clip icon instead of the Safari icon, and Safari opens to your home page instead of to the last page you visited.**

 You can even rearrange the icons so that your home page icon, instead of the Safari icon, appears in the dock (the bottom row that appears on every home screen).

Storing Files

A tiny Massachusetts software company known as Ecamm Network is selling an inexpensive piece of Mac OS X software that lets you copy files from your computer to your iPhone and copy files from the iPhone to a computer. (There is no Windows version.) Better still, you can try the $29.95 program PhoneView for a week before deciding whether you want to buy it. Go to www.ecamm.com to fetch the free demo.

In a nutshell, here's how it works. After downloading the software onto your Mac, double-click the program's icon to start it. To transfer files and folders to the iPhone (assuming there's room on the device), click the Copy to iPhone button on the toolbar and click to select the files you want to copy. The files are copied into the appropriate folder on the iPhone. Alternatively, you can drag files and folders from the Mac desktop or a folder into the PhoneView browser.

To go the other way and copy files from your iPhone to your computer, highlight the files or folders you want copied, and click the Copy from iPhone button on the toolbar. Select the destination on your Mac where you want to store the files and then click Save. You can also drag files and folders from the PhoneView file browser onto the Mac desktop or folder. Or you can double-click a file in the PhoneView browser to download it to your Mac's Documents folder.

If you need access to the files on your iPhone, or if you want to use your iPhone as a pseudo-hard disk, PhoneView is a bargain.

Create Ringtones for Free

It is relatively easy to create free iPhone ringtones with Apple's GarageBand application (which is bundled with every Mac). Start by launching GarageBand and creating a new Music project. Then do the following:

1. **Click the Media Browser button to reveal the media browser pane.**
2. **Click the disclosure triangle to reveal the contents of your iTunes library.**
3. **Click your iTunes music library to reveal its contents.**
4. **Click the song you want to turn into a ringtone and drag it onto the timeline.**

You can't use songs purchased from the iTunes store for ringtones because they are protected by Apple's digital rights management copy protection. GarageBand won't let you drag a protected song onto its timeline. So you can make ringtones only out of songs you've ripped yourself from CD or downloaded without rights management or other copy protection (such as MP3s from Amazon.com).

5. **Click the Cycle Region button to enable the Cycle Region.**

6. **Click in the middle of the Cycle Region and drag it to the portion of the song you want to use as your ringtone.**

7. **Fine-tune the beginning and end points by clicking and dragging the Cycle Region's left and right edges.**

   For best results, keep your ringtones under 30 seconds.

8. **Click the Play button to hear your work. When you're satisfied with it, choose Share⇨Send Ringtone to iTunes.**

The next time you sync, your new ringtone becomes available on your iPhone. To use it as your ringtone, tap Settings, tap Sounds, tap Ringtone, and then tap the ringtone in the list of available sounds. To associate it with a specific contact or contacts, find the contact in either the Contacts application or the Phone app's Contacts tab, tap Edit, tap Ringtone, and then tap the ringtone in the list of available sounds.

Take a Snapshot of the Screen

Press the Sleep/Wake button at the same time you press the Home button, but just for an instant. The iPhone grabs a snapshot of whatever is on the screen.

The picture lands in the iPhone's Camera Roll, from where you can synchronize it with your PC or Mac, include it in your Photo Stream, or assign it to a Shared Photo Stream.